Framed!

Solve an Intriguing Mystery and Master How to Make Smart Choices

Hari Singh, Ph.D.
Seidman School of Business

Give me a fruitful error anytime,
full of seeds, bursting with its own corrections.
You can keep your sterile truth for yourself.
—Vilfredo Pareto
Comment on Kepler, circa 1900

All that we know is nothing,
we are merely crammed waste-paper baskets,
unless we are in touch with that which laughs at all our knowing.
—D. H. Lawrence
Peace and War, Pansies, 1929

HRD PRESS, Inc.
Amherst, Massachusetts

Published by:
  HRD Press
  22 Amherst Road
  Amherst, MA 01002-9709
  800-822-2801 (U.S. and Canada)
  413-253-3488
  413-253-3490 (Fax)
  www.hrdpress.com

ISBN 0-87425-873-1

Editorial services by Sally M. Farnham
Typeset by Digital Publishing Solutions
Cover design by Eileen Klockars

Contents

Acknowledgments v

1. Fight or Flight? 1

2. Thriving on Stupidity 7

3. The Name of the Game is the Frame 21

4. Rewriting the Script 29

5. Weigh the Anchor without Rancor 37

6. Cause and Effect Is Hard to Detect 47

7. Gravitate to Your Own Risk Taste 59

8. Murder or Suicide? You Decide 67

9. Values and Facts 77

10. Shortcuts that Undercut 87

11. Dissect the Suspects 97

12. Track the Feedback 105

13. Verify the Alibi 113

14. Negotiate and Trust or Go Bust 121

15. WARS that Resolve 131

16. Tamper with the Anchor 139

17. Can You Spot Your Blots? 151

18. The Frame is the Name of the Game 161

19. What Means to What Ends? 169

20. A Look in the Mirror 177

Epilogue The Heart of the Matter 181

Appendix 1: Key Concepts/Questions 191

Appendix 2: Checklist 203

Appendix 3: Glossary 205

Appendix 4: References/A Conceptual Overview 209

Acknowledgments

When you begin to write a book, the debt you owe to a lot of people piles up quite easily. I am grateful to the following colleagues for reading the manuscript and providing feedback at various stages: Claudia Bajema, Dick Hall, Leigh Brownley, Gerry Simons, Richard Gonce, Vonnie Herrera, John Nader, Roger Frantz, Hugh Schwartz, Parvez Sopariwala, and Paul Thorsnes. Particularly comments from Morris Altman, Shlomo Maital, and Paul Zak have been very useful. MBA students in my decision-making course were extremely helpful with various suggestions.

The following colleagues were helpful in assembling the corporate reviewers: Marinus DeBruine, Dave Good, Paul Lane, Jaideep Motwani, John Reifel, Ben Rudolph, and Dan Wiljanen. Patricia Smith provided legal advice.

My appreciation goes out to the group of busy executives who agreed to read the book and provide valuable feedback: Dr. William Bayham, Peter Christie, Mohan Garde, Tim Good, Ivan Goldman, Randy Hansen, Pam Hoffman, Dr. David R. MacDonald, Richard Moskwa, William Van Oosterhout, Robert Tholl, Justin Vire, and Richard VanBelzen.

Madeleine Moore helped me with various formatting issues.

I am grateful to my family, Sheryl, Andrew, Jillian, and Jamie, for constant encouragement and feedback. My brother Dr. Raj Singh provided insights and advice about the Cicor case.

1
Fight or Flight?

Common sense is instinct. Enough of it is genius.
—George Bernard Shaw

One summer evening, Laura's life changed irrevocably. A split second decision—two lives at stake. Sometimes your whole life or everything that you hold dear can hinge on a single action—an action that doesn't allow the luxury of contemplation. All that you are and all that you know flows through you at that critical moment—your accumulated knowledge, your hopes, and your fears are all part of the instinctive response. The moment is frozen in time, you may go back and second-guess your decision many times over, but the world around you moves on. For Laura, this moment came when she was twenty-five years old; her sister Diane was twenty.

The day began like any other summer day in Chicago—hot, humid, and full of anticipation. As Laura recounted bits of the story to us on various occasions, she recalled looking forward to the new play opening at the Steppenwolf Theatre. Going with her sister was an added bonus.

The play ended around 11:00 at night. Diane and Laura stepped out from the theatre and walked toward Clark Street, looking for a late night snack. They were going back and forth about where to eat. As they turned a corner, Laura noticed that the sidewalk was well lit, but no one appeared to be around. In a moment, she sensed someone close behind them. She felt a hard object thrust into her back. The thick, hoarse voice had a drunken lisp.

"Don't move! Gimme your purse and put your hands out!"

Laura's mind raced. *What should I do first? No sudden moves for sure. I should do exactly what he says.* What she had always feared, what she had always thought unlikely, was actually happening to her.

"We're going to turn around slowly to give you our purses," she said. Then to her younger sister, "Diane, it will be okay." Laura heard an assenting grunt.

As Laura turned ever so slowly, she saw a tall, thin man. The hand that held the gun was quivering. A torn brown scarf covered his nose and mouth. When she held out her purse, he grabbed it with a sloppy swing. As he stumbled to take the purse from Diane, his own hand grazed his face, and the scarf slipped from his mouth. Laura noticed the stubby unshaven chin. His blue eyes narrowed. The grunt this time came out as a deep growl. Laura peered intently into his glassy eyes. The realization sliced through her consciousness in an instant. *He's going to kill us. My God! He's going to kill us!*

Laura remembered thinking, *What should I do*? She felt her pulse quicken. The fight or flight response had taken over. Suddenly, she heard her own voice shrieking, "Run, Diane, run!"

As Laura tried to move her legs, she heard the silencer on the gun whisper twice. Laura was aware of a police siren at a distance. Her legs wouldn't move fast enough. The last thing she remembered was the pavement rushing toward her face. . . .

Laura's head throbbed. The harsh light over the ER gurney penetrated her languid eyelids. She clearly heard voices.

"I'm afraid we have lost Diane," an authoritative voice said to someone. "But Laura will be okay. I have to go and talk to their relatives."

Laura couldn't open her eyes. She felt a crushing weight on her chest. All she kept thinking was: *What should I do? Run or fight?*

* * *

My brother interrupts the story.

"Larry, this incident is interesting but what has it got to do with the questions I have been asking? If I don't make the right calls on my decisions, I'll be dead meat! I swear! I'm so stressed out! What should I do?"

Chris, my kid brother, is pretending to pound his head on the wall. Actually, he isn't pretending—plaster is chipping off the wall! Chris towers over me; the acne on his cheeks is bright red. His deep-set brown eyes betray confusion. His onslaught of multi-level questions is unrelenting.

"You know I need to make up my mind about Linda. I love her and all that, but should I propose to her? I want to work in your company but my friends are all going to college. Should I go to college now? Maybe I should work in your company for a year and go to college later? I don't want you to decide for me. Just give me some input. What would you do in my place?" Chris's head thumps the plaster again.

He is pestering me with questions—I don't have very good responses. All I have are the sum of my life's experiences. I want him to learn how to seek his own answers. How can I pass on to him the lessons that I have learned from my mistakes? I realize things have changed for his generation. He will undoubtedly make his own mistakes, but I want him to know that his human frailty—his propensity to make errors—can be a source of enormous strength: that he can always pick up the pieces and reconfigure his own grail of learning and wisdom. I am not sure what will resonate in his consciousness, but I do know one thing: I have to capture his attention—otherwise the battle is already lost.

I try to build interest in the story. "This mugging incident about Laura is part of a larger story—a time when I learned how to cope with my own dilemmas. During one fateful spring season, while I was in the MBA program at St. Andrews, an exciting series of events transformed my world."

Chris is beginning to get interested in the story. He is almost nineteen years old, eleven years my junior. His behavior constantly reminds me of our dad—a father he has never really known. When Chris wants to ask an important question, he furrows his eyebrows, his voice grows softer, his physical presence more overpowering. He has to move around when he is pondering over something. He flexes his arms and legs while prowling back and forth. His restlessness fills the room with quick long moves. I remember father swaggering around the living room, speaking softly to my mother, making excuses to stay out of the house. Chris has our father's height, all six feet and two inches of him. I have my mother's clipped gait and small frame.

One cold spring day, when Chris was eight years old, our father left us. His departure did not come as a surprise. Although we had seldom seen him at home, he had set up generous allowances for all three of us. I was convinced he had calculated a formula in his mind for assuaging his guilt. Thousands of dollars could substitute for all the time he did not give us. Over the years, the thousands of dollars became several hundreds of thousands, but his letters and phone calls dried up. My mother suffered a nervous breakdown. Chris was sent to a boarding school in Lake Forest, a northern suburb of Chicago. I decided to continue my graduate studies at St. Andrews in Chicago, an elite private college. From there, I could keep an eye on my brother.

That memorable spring semester at St. Andrews sent my life spinning in a new direction. Many myths melted, along with the snow, that spring. I can't say I lost my innocence that year. My naiveté had slowly eroded as I watched my mother slip into a remote place. What I lost in Chicago that spring was my basic sense of order—a sense I had about the way things normally work. Somehow the world became a different place. I had to reconstruct a new sense of reality. The seasons of spring have asked me tough questions—I have tried to collect my strength, look for answers, and move on.

"Larry, would you marry Linda if you were in my place? Would you start working right now and defer going to college? Just give me some input, will you?" Chris brushes some plaster off his shirt.

I lean back and study Chris for a moment. I know what it is like, not having a father's guidance, to have a mother who is unable to provide convincing answers to my soul-searching questions. I want to be there for Chris as he moves into maturity. Four years ago, after that fateful spring at St. Andrews, Chris and I moved to San Francisco. I started my own software company. We now live in the same duplex apartment.

When I graduated with my MBA from St. Andrews, I thought I had a monopoly on wisdom. But all the information I had gathered from my courses was great for one thing—doing well on exams. Whether I could effectively use the information in my daily life was another matter. We were taught how to integrate concepts from different disciplines by case studies. But the case studies were sterile and static compared to the real dilemmas I faced. What mattered was not the information itself, but how it slowly brewed in my mind and increased my awareness—how that awareness led to bits and pieces of knowledge that I could apply to my ongoing problems.

Above all, I had to reflect on my own frailty and strength—to temper information with intuition and experience—in order to increase my awareness and knowledge. It may be a truism, but the most critical battles are fought within our own mind—that is where the story begins and ends—information is only a vehicle.

How do I wrap what I have learned into a neat package? What do I pass on to a nineteen year old that will endure? Again nostalgia flaps its wings and my thoughts fly back to that spring at St. Andrews. I could take Chris back to a different time and place—show him what I had learned—encourage him to develop a process for answering his own questions.

"Do you want to hear the rest of the story? The story will help you make up your own mind." I burrow into my favorite recliner and raise my feet. "You might find it interesting. I haven't told this entire story to anyone, Chris. I have saved it for you. It'll make more sense to you today, now that you're almost a grown man. Are you ready to hear it?"

"Since it's Friday evening and there is nothing to do—sure, what else is there? Does it have any action? It's not all philosophy, is it?"

"Not much philosophy, but some psychology will come up. Here, take a load off your feet. Sit down and relax while I get my journal. I need to refer to my notes. I was twenty-six years old at that time."

"Five years ago? You were getting your master's at St. Andrews, and I was in boarding school. Mom was going in and out of hospitals."

"Four years and three months to be exact. I have gone over those days in my mind again and again—those six days that transformed my world—that changed my perception of reality."

"All right, Larry, but just put some action in it, okay?" Chris sits against the overstuffed cushions on the sofa and curls his legs.

"The story is set in my favorite city—Chicago. It was an exciting time—a time when my soul mate Laura Armstrong and I discovered each other. I didn't know it then but I was about to encounter a series of nasty surprises. It was a time when a part of me died and another part of me had to be reborn—a season in spring that changed all my seasons...."

2
Thriving on Stupidity

Everyone is ignorant, only on different subjects.
—Will Rogers

Nine months after the mugging incident, Laura seemed to have recovered from the tragedy. She and I were MBA students at St. Andrews. We had both enrolled in Professor Martin Armstrong's infamous class for that spring quarter. Taking Professor Armstrong's decision-making course was considered a privilege for outstanding students. The professor talked at length to each student before deciding whether to add his or her name to the class roster. His seminar, *Thriving on Stupidity*, would have only fifteen students. The class would be held every weekday for three weeks, either in a classroom at St. Andrews or in the boardrooms of several major corporations.

Professor Armstrong had a Ph.D. not only in management strategy, but also in economics. He held an endowed chair in the Management Department. I was familiar with his reputation. He had published extensively on issues related to decision making. His articles appeared in the top business strategy and economics journals—a rare feat. In my first semester at St. Andrews, I took a class from Professor Armstrong. His provocative teaching style always kept me awake and interested in the discussion. I had built a rapport with him outside the classroom, talking to him on a variety of subjects.

Professor Armstrong had a zeal for looking at new ways to reduce poverty in the sub-Saharan countries of Africa. He had never married—books were his passion. His modest apartment was overflowing with books. Everyone talked about the huge bookcase between the toilet and the sink in the bathroom of his apartment. Professor Armstrong pushed books on his students all the time. "Read this book," he would say. "It won't hurt you!"

In those days, our wild imaginations and a blind faith in our unlimited potential constantly fueled our thinking. We could feel the blood surging through our veins, discovering new pathways. The ivy meandering over the walls of University Hall at St. Andrews always found a new path. Why couldn't we? We were never clear about where we were going—the wild ivy did not have a clue either! There was a limitless reservoir of energy, a limitless sense of possibility—but a limited sense of direction.

Professor Armstrong knew how to tap this boundless source of youthful energy. He understood our impatience and our need to do something—anything. He directed our energy to a noble pursuit: to test the limits of our knowledge and to discover more about the world and ourselves. He constantly quoted from Rudyard Kipling's poem "If."

"Recite these words slowly to yourself," he would say. "Let their exquisite taste, their timeless grandeur, and their intrinsic meaning roll off your tongue!

> 'If you can dream—and not make dreams your master,
> If you can think—and not make thoughts your aim;
> If you can meet with Triumph and Disaster
> And treat these two imposters just the same;
>
> If you can fill the unforgiving minute
> With sixty seconds' worth of distance run,
> Yours is the Earth and everything that's in it
> And—which is more—you'll be a Man, my son!' "

Professor Armstrong could combine poetry, psychology, economics, and management into a unique blend—a recipe that would create an invigorating perspective on a complex problem. He assigned a topic and expected us to research it thoroughly. Once we understood the problem completely, he forced us to explain it in simple terms. He called these activities "mind-bending exercises."

"Push your body to the limit," he pointed out, "Go to the gym and work your heart out. Then go to the library—only if you're excited—only if you want to instill each unforgiving minute with sixty seconds of new knowledge. A supple mind in an energized body! What more could any of us want?"

How can I describe St. Andrews? The school is a cluster of regal buildings, guarded by old trees, nesting in grassy meadows—a small river runs through the campus. St. Andrews is a collection of different sounds: friends laughing with each other; teachers intoning in their baritone voices; students flopping their heels on the beaten cobblestone paths; and if you listen closely, you can always hear the cascading sound of the river. The river follows you wherever you go—meandering between buildings. Students had dubbed the river "Plato"—constantly seeking wisdom. Plato emptied into a lake that students had renamed "Aristotle." Plato was always looking for Aristotle—curving past the grassy meadows, trying to find its way.

Each season cast a different mask on the campus—sometimes white, at other times, green or reddish brown. But the underlying personality—the pace and bustle of campus life—always had the same level of excitement. Every semester, the boundless energy and vibrancy of St. Andrews renewed itself—new students, new ideas, new choices, and always new possibilities.

As a student, you soak in the life at St. Andrews: the sounds, the backdrops, the new opportunities, and the constant learning. Before you realize it, the school becomes a part of you. It changes you in more ways than you can imagine. As I look back at my life at St. Andrews, what grabs me is an acute sense of nostalgia for those days. Somehow the campus life, the exciting relationship with Laura, the forging of lifelong friendships are refracted back through a youthful prism of glorious memories. Nostalgia has a way of treasuring the memories, of adding an element of magic to even mundane events. Without question, those were the best years of my life.

When I entered the classroom, Professor Armstrong was making his stump speech. His blue eyes were wide and inquisitive. He rubbed his gray beard with one hand; the other hand chopped the air.

"Why is this course called *Thriving on Stupidity*? Let's face it. When trying to make decisions, we make dumb mistakes all the time. We have to tame the beast that lives within—the beast that feeds on our impulses and obscures clear thinking. If I had to choose one thing to do well, it would be to learn from my mistakes. Once I'm adept at doing that, I won't continue to make the same mistakes again and again. Eventually, I'll run out of mistakes. I'll be on the road to good decision making!"

As Professor Armstrong's thin frame vibrated with his booming voice, I saw that many students had quizzical looks on their faces. They were wondering, *What's this guy up to? Why is he talking about making mistakes?* But we were all under Professor Armstrong's spell as he spun a web from different directions. I was familiar with his teaching technique. "Provoke, stimulate, agitate, even confuse them," he would say. "Above all, make them think! If one person sleeps or nods off in my class, I have failed!"

Professor Armstrong started another strand. "This class can't inoculate you against bad decisions. Avoiding bad choices altogether is impossible. One less faulty decision, however, is an improvement. Nobody has a monopoly over wisdom. We're all competing to reduce our stupidity. We'll try to learn a process that acknowledges our limitations, a process that opens new windows to our minds. These windows will look within as well as without. We can use this method to take advantage of other people's stupidity and capitalize on their mistakes."

As he spun his web, I could see that every student was captivated by his provocative style. Well, almost every student. At the back of the class, Stewart Anderson moved his laptop around his desk, trying to find the perfect spot for his computer. Stewart and his laptop had become one symbiotic being. Most of the time, they would conspire with each other in a hushed tone. At other times, he used the laptop as a modified pillow. Stewart found the ideal spot for his laptop. He rested his elbows on the machine and supported his chin with his hands. His eyelids drooped and he swayed a little. Then he did the unforgivable in Professor Armstrong's class—he yawned!

Professor Armstrong's blazing eyes settled on him. "Stewart! Having made decisions all your life, can you tell us the most important component in the decision-making process?"

Stewart adjusted his tie awkwardly and looked around for help. He mumbled, "I think all aspects are important, uh... especially the method by how you decide, uh...."

Professor Armstrong's sarcasm was legendary. "Uh, uh, I don't think we are, uh, making the right point, uh," he mimicked. By this time, Stewart had run out of words, and looked dejectedly at the floor.

Clara Starr, a precocious and inquisitive student, came to the rescue. "Professor? Perhaps the most important component of decision making is *how* we arrive at a decision."

"That's quite good, Clara," Professor Armstrong acknowledged. "The most important aspect is how we 'frame' the decision. By *frame* I mean the decision maker's conceptualization of his problem, the way he chooses to think about a particular issue. What information should he take into account? Is he clear about the objective and the range of alternatives? Has he ruled out some options prematurely? A decision maker has to draw a boundary around an issue when he is framing."

Clara listened intently. She reveled in supporting underdogs. Her petite five-foot frame would bristle with indignation at some injustice. She always volunteered for different causes: animal rights, freedom in Tibet, child abuse. We called her "our social conscience." Clara always asked questions in class. Now something still disturbed her, and she raised her hand. "How do we know if we have the right frame?"

Professor Armstrong stood very still. "You have hit upon a critical question, Clara, a question that doesn't have a good answer. While making a decision, it's difficult to know for sure if we have the right frame. When we're inside a frame, it appears solid and foolproof. But a frame always simplifies and thereby distorts reality. A minor change in the way we frame an issue can significantly alter our perception of the problem. Framing involves a dilemma. In order to simplify, we have to frame, but once we have framed, we may inadvertently exclude relevant information or options. So frame the issue with imagination and humility. This is the most important part of the decision-making process. *The name of the game is the frame."*

Professor Armstrong transformed every important concept into a slogan. He would repeat these invented phrases until they echoed relentlessly in our heads. He would ordain, "Repeat this mantra until you are unable to avoid mumbling it in your sleep!"

Clara had another question: "Since most of us are planning to work in a corporation, will you provide more economics and business examples?"

Professor Armstrong ran his fingers through his beard. "The problems you will face as an executive can't be confined to any single discipline. As a manager, you have to understand and operate in a complex environment. Many factors that are directly or indirectly related to business will come into play: How you frame an issue, whether you can determine cause and effect, the way you deal with risk, and your ability to avoid psychological biases are all relevant. You have to apply these concepts to a wide variety of problems—reflect on their generality—ensure they become part of your thinking process."

I glanced at Laura sitting in the chair in front of me. I recalled the wind-swept day I met her for the first time. As a freshman, I signed up for a tennis class to get easy credits. I was waiting for the class to begin, standing alongside the tennis courts, when suddenly I saw stars! These dim flickering lights were all over my eyes. It took me a moment to realize that a fast tennis ball had hit me in the head. The next thing I saw was Laura's face floating over mine.

"I'm sorry! I lost control of the ball. Are you all right?" Laura's voice sounded genuinely concerned.

Even through the foggy blur, I appreciated her bright hazel eyes. She had an even, angular face with a small preppie nose. Her voice had a delicate lilt. As I stood up slowly, I noticed Laura had a small, well-proportioned frame. A sharp pain pulsated through my neck—I was not all right. The pain at the base of my neck lasted for three weeks, but it was worth it. Laura started talking to me during class, and I asked her to play a game of tennis with me. I lost badly, but during the entire evening the smile never left my face!

After the tennis class, we started dating regularly. Although we did not live together, we were always discovering new things about each other. Somehow, the space within us and between us had a way of stretching and enveloping us in its embrace. It was as if we lived in a bubble—we could feed off each other's energy. Even now in the presence of all the others in class, as I sat behind Laura, I could sense her energy—the space around her had a unique vibrancy. I noticed her shoulders were arched a little higher—something was bothering her.

Professor Armstrong's voice jolted me back to the classroom. "The name of the game is the frame. When you're framing, be a *contrarian*—always ask uncomfortable, probing questions that are different from your prior beliefs. Can you look at the problem from a different angle? In a corporate setting, your subordinates are likely to tell you what they think you want to hear. Ask them questions that are contrary to what you believe may be happening. In this way, you may find out what they really think. Don't bask in the comfort of your initial impressions. Actively question your presumptions."

Professor Armstrong rubbed his beard in an agitated manner. I sensed he was coming to a major point.

"We will cast a wide net to capture the complexity of framing choices. Our strategy is called FACTNET, an acronym for seven critical concepts for decision making:

<u>F</u>raming or conceptualizing the issue creatively

<u>A</u>nchoring or relying on reference points

<u>C</u>ause and effect

<u>T</u>astes for risk preference and the role of chance

<u>N</u>egotiation and the importance of trust

<u>E</u>valuating decisions by a process

<u>T</u>racking relevant feedback."

Professor Armstrong underlined the first letter of each sentence. "Don't worry if you are unaware of what any of these words mean. Ignorance has its advantages: I won't have to bother about your preconceived misconceptions. I can stuff your mind with the right concepts. Within a few weeks, you'll be mumbling these words in your sleep. You'll be assigned topics to explore and research. I don't tolerate sloppy work!"

Clara raised her hand, "How much time should we spend on each decision?"

"Time is our most valuable asset. We should spend more time and effort on a decision that has greater consequences. That begs a second question: How much time should we devote to each stage in the process of decision making? Framing the problem is the most critical part of the process. For important decisions, don't jump in and make a rash choice. Step back! View the mental landscape. Consider alternatives with an open mind. Actively question your presumptions. The subsequent stages of the decision process must rest on a solid foundation."

By this time, three students at the back of the class were behaving as if they had a sudden attack of hemorrhoids: They were shifting around in their seats and occasionally glancing at the clock. Professor Armstrong knew when our attention span was running out. He methodically wrote our assignment on the white board and left.

On our way out, I asked Laura, "Are you okay? You looked as if your mind was on something other than Professor Armstrong's lecture."

"I'll be all right," she sighed. Then her tone of voice changed, and I could tell she wanted to change the subject. "I hope Professor Armstrong won't treat me differently than he does the other students just because I'm his niece. I know *he* won't, but I hope other people won't change their behavior toward me."

"I don't think you'll have any problems." I noticed her left hand trembled as she held her thick stack of books. I wondered if Diane's murder was finally taking its toll on Laura. Although Laura talked about the incident frequently, she rarely mentioned Diane. I knew Laura had been very close to her sister, but whenever I mentioned Diane, Laura would change the subject. Should I press the issue?

"Hey!" Laura's mood abruptly changed. "Want to come to a real exciting reception tonight?" she rolled her eyes, letting me know the affair would be anything but exciting. "The Armstrong Foundation is having its annual awards dinner. Unfortunately, I have to go."

Going to a formal reception was bad enough. An awards function was worse. I would have to keep smiling and clapping on cue—but Laura was asking.

"Sure! Beats preparing for tomorrow's class."

* * *

Laura and I strolled along the banks of Plato. The sharp wind made us nestle against each other, and the cascading water had a soothing effect. We followed Plato to the Commons cafeteria. There appeared to be a commotion going on inside.

"What's happening?" I asked Stewart. He was having a smoke outside the Commons, while peering through the windows. As we approached, he hurriedly put out his cigarette.

"Paul Gerber is having a violent outburst. Let's go in and watch the show."

As we entered the Commons, I heard a loud snapping sound. Paul Gerber had picked up a wooden chair and was banging it on the table. His face had a vacant, faraway look, and his eyes narrowed with intense concentration. The chair hit the table over and over with tremendous force.

"How did this start?" I asked Stewart, who was observing Paul with fascination.

"I don't know. I heard Paul yelling from outside. Apparently he was having an argument with Clara. In the middle of the conversation, he got up and started destroying the chair."

Clara stood on one side with a throng of students. She appeared to be in shock. Paul Gerber had broken the chair into three pieces, then he threw the pieces on the floor and stomped on them. Paul was breathing hard with the exertion. Oblivious to the watching crowd, he kept breaking the pieces down with unrelenting force. When the chair lay on the floor in a dozen pieces, Paul abruptly stopped. Without saying a word, he stomped out.

"Clara, are you all right?" Laura asked.

"I'm fine. Can you believe this? I was having a small disagreement with him when he got up and started wrecking the chair," Clara shook her head.

Laura put an arm around Clara. "You look a little shaky. Why don't you come with us to the library?"

After finishing at the library, I went to see Professor Armstrong. I noticed a new African mask on his office wall. The penetrating eyes of the mask were balanced by an ambiguous smile on the wooden face. The mask seemed to watch over the office—all-knowing and vigilant. Professor Armstrong was facing his computer screen when I knocked.

"Come in, Larry, it's good to have you in class again."

He kept scanning his monitor. As I sneaked a glance at the screen, a news headline jumped out: "AIDS DEVASTATES COUNTRIES IN SUB-SAHARAN REGION."

"Thanks, I'm enjoying the class." I unloaded my backpack. "I hope we can continue our discussions outside the classroom."

Professor Armstrong turned and looked at me. "I like your questions, Larry. You have an inquisitive mind. You may not know the right answers, but you know where to look. That's a good start."

Compliments from Professor Armstrong were rare and always qualified. He indicated a chair, and I sat down. "I wanted to ask you about some references on rationality. I'm discovering that economists and psychologists have different perspectives on what they regard as 'rational' behavior. In economics, a person is deemed to be *rational* if he makes an optimal decision by using all available information. Economists don't focus on the process of decision making or on the potential errors in judgment. On the other hand, in cognitive psychology, an individual is *rationalizing*, always trying to cope with more information. Individual perceptions and cognitive limitations are viewed as part of the decision-making process."

Professor Armstrong nodded. "That's a good distinction. Economists look for *long-term, stable outcomes.* At the aggregate level, most individual differences become progressively less important. Given time, with continuous learning, individual decisions tend to approach optimal outcomes. Economists focus on the final stable results that tend to increase satisfaction or utility. On the other hand, cognitive psychologists investigate decision making as a *fallible process that can be improved.*"

"How do we reconcile the two approaches?"

"In our decision-making class, we'll blend both views. We'll recognize the psychological viewpoint that individuals are fallible and rationalizing. In our daily lives, we all succumb to psychological traps and biases. It's important that we learn how to recognize and avoid them. We'll take advantage of several systematic procedures and strive to be objective in our decision-making process. As an executive, you will need to reconcile conflicting information and avoid psychological biases. I'll send you a list of references by e-mail."

Professor Armstrong turned toward his computer. I picked up my backpack, but before I could leave he continued. "Here's something to think about. Let's assume that most people are rational and well informed. Consider two questions for our next meeting: Why do we have heated arguments on many controversial topics such as abortion, executive accountability, and drug use? How can we develop a better consensus on these divisive issues?"

The professor liked to answer questions by raising other questions. He would throw these questions at me in our conversations. I would go to the library and try to dig up some answers. That would set the stage for our next discussion. I was not yet armed with any citations or readings about reaching consensus.

"Send me the list of references about rationality," I said on my way out. "I'll get back to you on these questions."

Professor Armstrong was already working on his computer. He waved his hand. "Bend your mind in the library, but make sure you go to the gym first."

* * *

At the Daley Center Plaza, a huge tent had been set up with outdoor heating. The movers and shakers mobbed around the *Picasso*. I had seen most of their faces on the pages of the *Chicago Tribune*. The Armstrong Foundation was a charitable organization financed by the family trust fund. John Armstrong, the elder brother of Professor Armstrong, had made his fortune as a meat packer. He had multiplied his wealth in the commodity futures market.

John Armstrong believed strongly that a lot of money is not good for young people. After his death, his billions of dollars were bequeathed to a fund managed by a board of trustees. Donald

Armstrong, Laura's elder brother, was the president of the board. Professor Armstrong was the vice-president. John's three children, Laura, Donald, and Diane, had she lived, would have no direct access to the money until they were thirty-five years old. At that time, they would share equally in the vast Armstrong fortune. The Armstrong children were given a generous annual allowance for living expenses. In the meanwhile, the board donated the ongoing earnings of the Armstrong Fund to a variety of domestic causes.

As I walked in, feeling uncomfortable in my rented tuxedo, I saw Laura in a formal blue dress. She was waiting in the reception line with Professor Armstrong, Donald, and the other board members.

Laura whispered as she took me aside, "Martin is fuming about the board vote."

Laura used the professor's first name regularly when we were off campus. "Martin asked the board to allocate some money for projects in developing countries, but the board wants to keep the money in Chicago. What better way to please local politicians?"

Laura did not have to fill me in on the rest. I could see that the professor was angry. Whenever he was trying to keep his temper in check he would put his left hand deep in his pocket. When he rose to make his welcome speech his hand never came out of the pocket. His voice was calm and measured.

"Ladies and Gentlemen," he began. "As the Armstrong Foundation announces the awards for this year, I'm reminded of the pioneering spirit of John Armstrong. He was a man with strong shoulders in a city of broad shoulders. John's compassion did not know any boundaries. During the cold war, he gave generously to noble causes all over the world. We reward the recipients tonight for their tenacity and hard work, their ability to think of new ways to help the neediest in our great city."

Trust Professor Armstrong to make a point about compassion without borders. Laura grabbed my arm and steered me toward her brother. "Donald, I want you to meet Larry Rowe."

Donald turned and looked at me as he spoke. "Larry who? I didn't catch the name with all this traffic noise."

"Larry Rowe. You know Larry don't you?" There was a hint of a challenge in her voice. Donald had met me several times before. He was playing one of his games.

Donald smiled, "Ah yes, Larry. Larry Rowe. Professor Armstrong's great student. How are you, Larry?" Donald was already looking at a state senator as he spoke. His mind had moved on.

Laura shrugged her shoulders. "I don't know what to say. I haven't figured out my brother yet. I'm sorry, Larry."

"Nothing to be sorry about, Laura. Let's just try to have a good time."

Someone gently squeezed my elbow. Phillip Myers was standing next to me. Phil was tall with a stocky frame. A bemused smile always played on his lips. His alert eyes complemented a sharp Roman nose.

"Phil! What are you doing here?" I asked.

"My mentor, Shawn Douglas, wanted me to scope out the security arrangements and meet some bigwigs." Phil scanned the windows of the tall Cook County administration building across the street. He hugged Laura warmly.

Phil and I went back a long way. We grew up together in Lake Forest. In high school, Phil had been voted the student "most likely to succeed." His favorite television show was *Columbo*. For hours, he would don a worn-out overcoat, and act out Columbo's lines. We thought he might wind up an actor, but he enrolled in the police academy instead and became a detective.

Phil had finished training and was assigned to work with Shawn Douglas, the chief detective of Precinct Nine. Shawn showed an avid interest in Phil's training. As Phil progressed through his career, he continued to take classes at St. Andrews. Laura, Phil, and I had spent countless hours hanging out together on and off campus. The three of us could manufacture a conversation from nothing and let it go on for hours.

"Do you want to drive out with me for Professor Armstrong's class tomorrow?" he asked. "I couldn't make class today, maybe you can fill me in." His request jolted my memory. Tomorrow's class was to be held at a downtown corporate office.

"Pick me up at 9:00," I replied. Phil was now peering at the windows of the courthouse office building. These cops never stop looking. As I moved on to talk to Laura, I saw that Professor Armstrong had finally pulled his hand out from his pocket. He was backslapping a local congressman. Donald Armstrong was huddled in a corner, talking heatedly with three corporate executives. One of the executives was quite agitated. I wondered what was going on.

3
The Name of the Game is the Frame

If the only tool you have is a hammer,
you tend to see every problem as a nail.
—Abraham Maslow

A s Phil drove toward downtown Chicago from the west side, we took in the spectacular city landscape. An early spring mist lingered around the shoulders of the tall buildings. On the far side, the John Hancock Tower looked out toward Lake Michigan. In the foreground, the smaller buildings in the Loop huddled around the Sears Tower, with its two vertical antennas. The EL metro snaked around the downtown buildings. Phil listened attentively to my recap of the previous class.

"What did the acronym FACTNET stand for?" asked Phil. "Wait—don't tell me. Framing, anchoring, cause and effect, taste for risk, negotiation and cooperation, and the last one is tracking feedback. What's before tracking feedback? Something that starts with an E."

"*E* is for evaluating the decision, Phil. He said we would discuss several ways to make decisions. One thing he emphasized was not to lose 'frame control'."

"What did he mean by *frame control*?"

"During framing, it's important to look at a problem from different vantage points and take time to explore all options. For instance, if our ultimate goal is to increase market share by 10 percent, we may explore many options: acquire new patents, develop improved products, and fine tune our marketing techniques. We should actively pursue this wider set of possibilities but also remain focused on our goal of increasing market opportunities.

We may need to cut our prices and profit margins in the short term to increase our market share over the long haul. We lose frame control if we get side tracked by the lure of short-term profits. It's important to have a flexible frame, but it's even more important to achieve our objective."

Phil went on a different track. "Donald Armstrong seemed agitated last night. I have been hearing rumors that he's about to fire three employees."

"And last year seven employees left en masse," I said.

Fifteen years ago, Professor Armstrong began a consulting practice about decision-making strategies. In a few years his firm, Global Options, Inc., had become renowned for helping top managers develop winning corporate strategies. Ten years later, he brought his nephew, Donald Armstrong, as a partner into the firm. Donald had graduated with a double masters degree in psychology and business from Boston College.

"Donald has an interesting management style," Phil explained. "His concept of teamwork is, 'If you don't claw your way to the top, you're on your way out.' That kind of fierce competition breeds animosity. He actually believes that this hand-to-hand combat feeds the creative juices. On the other hand, Professor Armstrong plays the good cop, soothing bruised egos. Somehow the firm has thrived with this dual approach— the employees are always on edge, trying to give their best performance."

Donald's reputation as an executive who gets results came at a price. He was regarded as frosty, manipulative, and ruthless. The word around the firm was that he enjoyed firing employees. But Donald was not a traditional corporate type. His attire always consisted of a Hawaiian shirt, jeans, and pair of designer sneakers. As CEO of Global Options, Inc., Donald did not believe in a rigid corporate structure. Everyone talked to everybody; nobody made formal reports. The lack of a formal structure, in a small firm with forty employees, enabled him to pull strings from many different directions.

Professor Armstrong and Donald provided one simple thing to corporations: A new way of looking at old problems. How do you spawn fresh successful ideas? The recipe was to develop competing frames. The name of the game is the frame, Professor Armstrong had pointed out to us repeatedly. Global Options was a money-making machine that had put this idea into practice.

Students were trying to find their seats when we entered the conference room of Global Options—GO as the employees called it. I noticed that the seating arrangement was similar to a theatre-in-the-round. Donald sat in the middle with three other persons. Ten chairs faced the center on each of the four sides. Professor Armstrong directed us to the chairs on the sides.

"We're going to play a framing game," the professor began. "We'll analyze a specific problem confronting an American firm, Premier Advanced Cardio Enterprises (PACE). The company has come to GO with a specific problem. Donald and PACE executives will present the company's viewpoint. All of you will be required to research the issue based on publicly available information. We have divided the class into three frame teams. Each frame team has students from a variety of backgrounds. Donald will explain the rationale of the frame teams."

Donald Armstrong rose from his seat. The smirk on his face matched the arrogant tone of his voice. "Have you noticed that where you stand is generally based on where you sit? I mean that literally and figuratively. Literally, your seating arrangement within a frame team will influence your thinking. Figuratively, we are trapped in our own mental structures. When you undergo graduate training to be an economist or an engineer, you do more than learn about a subject area. You develop a specific mental structure for thinking—a frame that compels you to look at every-thing in a specific way."

"That's not necessarily a bad thing, is it?" Phil asked.

"Did I say it was a bad thing? If an engineer doesn't know engineering, how else would he solve a mechanical problem? But we have to recognize that when we're trained in a discipline, our mind orients to a specific way of thinking that can be limiting. That's why we have organized frame teams with students from a variety of backgrounds so that you can interact and try to think outside your normal frame. Each frame team has students from different disciplines—economics, psychology, statistics, and business."

Professor Armstrong interjected: "We want to explore a wide set of options before we start drawing boundaries around a problem. Try to think outside your conventional box. Donald will explain what the representatives of PACE have to say. They have a problem that needs to be addressed. We'll have a friendly competition among the frame teams to come up with solutions. This will be an interesting way to learn about some of the general issues in framing. Are you ready?"

Most students had found their designated seats in a frame team. Some students nodded. "Good!" Professor Armstrong said, "Let the games begin."

Donald gazed at all the expectant faces around him. He adjusted the collar of his Hawaiian shirt, hunched his shoulders, and tapped the table with his pen. For a few long minutes, we heard only the irritating tapping. When he spoke, his arrogant tone was gone, but the smirk remained. He began in a low, hesitant voice, feigning confusion.

"Welcome. We want your help in trying to solve a vexing problem that will cost PACE more than a billion dollars this year. Consider item one: Three years ago, PACE began selling a powerful new medicine under the brand name of Cicor. This medicine reduces the risk of heart attacks. The drug showed promising results in medical trials. Cicor appeared to be safe and very effective. This new wonder drug was expected to generate annual sales of one billion dollars within a few years."

Donald paused, allowing the words to sink in. He picked up his pen and began the tapping again—three sharp, deliberate taps punctuated by a self-indulgent gaze around the room.

"Consider item two: PACE had to withdraw Cicor from the market three years later due to the unexpected deaths of several patients. The immediate sales loss is expected to be almost a billion dollars for this year. The share price of the company has dropped 30 percent within a few days. The ultimate loss due to forgone sales, legal fees, and financial settlements with the patients or their relatives will be several billion dollars. What went wrong? PACE has approached GO to search for imaginative solutions. The objective is to avoid a similar situation for other drugs that they are developing. Perhaps they need to revise their decision-making procedures. Help us solve this billion dollar corporate mystery."

Donald stopped abruptly and examined the tip of his pen. John Scott, a psychology major, spoke up. He was the captain of the ice hockey team. John believed his strongest asset on the field was his psychological insights. "If you don't beat them inside your head," he would say, "you've already lost!" John had a way of changing the pitch of his voice suddenly to attract attention. He called it his "waking up technique." We called him "Roller Coaster John."

"Why don't you begin by sketching out the problem," John suggested. "Then we can pester you with questions. That's part of the framing exercise, isn't it—asking uncomfortable questions?"

Donald continued to examine his pen. The arrogance had crept back into his tone. "Yes, by all means ask probing questions. PACE is a large U.S. company specializing in new medical treatments and high-tech cardio equipment. Their annual sales exceed five billion dollars. Cicor, their most promising product, is a statin drug that demonstrated dramatic results in experimental trials. Clinical studies showed that average reductions in low-density lipoprotein—that's bad cholesterol—were around 30 percent. Reductions of triglycerides of 40 percent were observed. For patients with elevated levels of bad cholesterol and triglycerides, Cicor can significantly reduce the risk of heart attacks by 40 to 60 percent."

John raised his hand, "Please stop right there. You're going too fast and using many technical words. What are triglycerides and bad cholesterol? What are statins? How does the medicine reduce the risk of heart disease?"

Donald glanced at a man sitting next to him. The person cleared his throat.

"Excuse me, my name is Roger Dykstra. I'm responsible for monitoring the benefits and safety of Cicor for PACE. I have a background in medicine and statistics. High levels of triglycerides and bad cholesterol in the blood stream are associated with clogging of arteries that eventually contributes to a heart attack. Statins are a remarkable class of drugs that inhibit the production of bad cholesterol and triglycerides. Consequently, statins prevent buildup of plaque inside artery walls. There are several statin drugs marketed under brand names such as Zocor®, Pravachol®, and Lipitor®. Cicor is another promising statin."

John followed up, "Thanks for the explanation. Doesn't PACE have any sense about what went wrong? What's the company's take on the problem?"

Donald put his pen down and looked at John, as if noticing him for the first time. "PACE has some initial conjectures. The problem is that each department approaches the issue from their own frame. The research department feels that not enough trials were performed to ascertain the safe dosage of the drug. The marketing department believes that doctors and patients were not educated about the risks and benefits of the medicine. The public relations department thinks that the unfair negative publicity is to blame for the company's huge losses. The different views of the various departments aren't surprising—each is constrained by their own frame. We have to…"

Stewart Anderson looked up from his laptop and interrupted Donald: "Doesn't PACE spend a lot of money on research? Are they under pressure to recover this money?"

Donald curled his lips to indicate his distaste for the interruption. He looked away from Stewart.

"Yes, PACE spends a great deal on research. They have spent fifteen billion dollars over twenty years to find effective ways of reducing the risk of heart disease. The FDA—the Food and Drug Administration—is continuously monitoring their research trials under rigorous guidelines. PACE wants to provide a safe and effective medicine that has demonstrable benefits to patients."

Professor Armstrong picked up the conversation, "One thing GO realized early on is that at this initial framing stage, we need to generate competing ideas. Otherwise, we may inevitably focus on a narrow set of alternatives and solutions. In order to get to the bottom of this mystery, it's important for all of you to ask probing questions."

* * *

My brother interrupts the story.

"Gee, Larry! This Cicor problem is interesting, but what does it have to do with changing your life? Why are you telling me about this class

exercise?" Chris is not sure that this story on Friday night is a good idea after all.

"I want you to have some background about the Cicor case. We're going to use it to understand and apply several important concepts. I'm only giving you about 20 percent...the best 20...of what we talked about."

"I think I understand what you're saying about the importance of a frame. When I come to you with a problem, you pester me with annoying and disturbing questions. Now I know why—you're trying to make sure that I look at a problem from several viewpoints, aren't you?"

"You're right, Chris, that's exactly what I do, even at the cost of sometimes driving you crazy. This whole thing about a frame reminds me of a simple folk tale. Three blind men went to 'see' an elephant. One man felt the belly with his hands, and came away with the impression that an elephant was like a wall. Another man felt the trunk, and thought the elephant was similar to a python. The third blind man wrapped his hands around the leg. He was sure the elephant resembled the trunk of a tree."

"That's a funny example, Larry. We need to see the big picture don't we?"

"Yes, Chris, we need to conceptualize our problems on a broader stage. Try to use our imagination not only to conjure up realistic images, but also to broaden our outlook by looking aggressively for new information. Each blind man came away confident that he knew what an elephant was like. We're like these blind men when we frame a complicated problem. We tend to view the problem through a narrow frame. We can walk away thinking we have the right frame, but in reality, our frame could be limiting our peripheral vision—distorting our reality. I have found that in the early stages of decision making at my firm, it is productive to brainstorm on a regular basis to ensure we have looked at all the angles. We try to aggressively look for new information to contradict our current frame."

"Stop your lecture for a minute and tell me about Laura. What was she like?"

"Laura and I had a chemistry that's difficult to describe. We had a similar mental outlook about most things. We empathized with each other's viewpoint. Silence was comfortable between us. On rare occasions, when we disagreed, sparks would fly. But there was no tension in

our arguments, only vigorous debate. My surroundings felt different when I was with Laura. I had an acute sense of awareness—a feeling that the contours of our world had become soft, the edges somehow more pliable. Anything could change its shape and excite us. Even the most mundane chores became adventures...."

"*Gee, Larry! Now you sound like a poet! You've been reading too many of those old Victorian poems. I meant what kinds of movies she liked. What kinds of songs? Don't get mushy on me.*"

"*Sorry, Chris. I just wanted to give you a sense of my relationship with Laura. At that time, though, something was happening to Laura— I didn't know exactly what was bothering her. But let me return to the story. I want to talk about another student. His name was Raj Kumar...."*

4
Rewriting the Script

Doubt is not a very pleasant status,
But certainty is a ridiculous one.
—Voltaire

Raj Kumar seldom showed any excitement. Perhaps his Indian culture had programmed him that way. Maybe it was a side effect of his daily meditations. He claimed that one hour of meditation was equivalent to three hours of sleep, so he slept four hours and meditated for two. Whenever we saw him, he looked disheveled. But his eyes were alive, glistening, dark brown, always darting back and forth.

Raj raised his hand and asked: "What exactly does the Cicor case teach us about framing?"

Professor Armstrong admonished, "Don't jump the gun. Try to find out for yourself. Sometimes a client may come to us with a set of questions. Our main contribution could be to *identify a different set of questions* that may resolve the underlying problem more effectively. Before the 1980s, American automakers asked a basic question: What's the minimum number of cars we need to produce of a particular model to make reasonable profits? This question is important because changes in technology and consumer tastes demand building different models at short notice. But changing the assembly line to make a new model is expensive because of the shutdown time during changeover. In order to reduce costs, auto manufacturers rarely introduced new models."

"That seems reasonable," Raj pointed out.

"Yes Raj, you're right, it seemed reasonable. The frame appeared intact and sound from the inside," Professor Armstrong answered as he curved his hands into a circle to illustrate. "Japanese manufacturers, however, asked a new question: How can we redesign the whole assembly line in order to make model changes more quickly and less expensively? Eventually, changeover was whittled down to a few minutes compared to several hours. The issue had been framed in a new way. The result was a more efficient and lean manufacturing process. During framing, we have to actively question and challenge the conventional bounds of thinking."

Professor Armstrong walked toward the center of the room. Donald was again preoccupied with his pen, rotating it slowly between his fingers. I was not sure if he was even listening to the discussion.

Professor Armstrong resumed: "Sometimes we end up kicking ourselves for not thinking about an issue from the right perspective. Let me illustrate with a personal example. About five years ago, I was feeling sad for no apparent reason. There was no sign of bad health, no death in the family, my job performance seemed adequate. And yet this vague feeling of sadness wouldn't go away. After reviewing many possibilities, I concluded that this sadness came from a realization that I wouldn't be able to do some things I had wanted to do in my life."

Everyone listened with rapt attention. This rare personal glimpse of Professor Armstrong had started right in the middle of the GO pit! He continued, "I had fond notions of becoming a successful author or directing an international relief agency. Would meeting these lofty objectives really make me happy? It was hard to say. At least, I was trying to frame the issue in a broad context and develop viable alternatives. I had to identify the source of my sadness. Otherwise, all the alternatives would lead only to superficial solutions. To frame correctly, we have to be honest with ourselves and ask the right questions."

"So what did you decide?" I asked.

"That will have to wait for another day. There's a point to my personal confession. We have to evaluate ourselves candidly. While framing an issue, we need to recognize our ignorance. Although framing is the most important part of the decision-making exercise, there's no foolproof procedure for framing."

"Are there any kind of guidelines?" Raj asked.

"Here are a few points to remember when you develop a frame:

- Identify your objectives clearly.

- Be candid about your ignorance; aggressively seek new information.

- Actively question your presumptions.

- Don't draw narrow boundaries; consider a wider set of alternatives.

"We'll discuss a host of important issues with the Cicor mystery. Let me start by giving you a clue. How do reference points influence PACE's strategy for Cicor? Put on your thinking caps and approach this puzzle with imagination."

We had been talking about framing for more than an hour. Professor Armstrong suggested some Web sites before adjourning.

* * *

The Commons cafeteria exhibited a false sense of calm and peace. Since our decision-making class met every day at an odd time, we sat in the cafeteria while other classes were in session. Between classes the cafeteria became a war zone of competing noises—students raising their voices, the clattering of dishes, and the ringing of the cash register made any decent conversation impossible. We were enjoying the brief truce between classes.

As we munched our snacks, Laura said unexpectedly, "I think I know how Professor Armstrong resolved his personal problem. He went to Sudan five years ago to do volunteer work over the summer. Since then, he's been going to different parts of Africa and Asia every summer for some kind of relief effort. In fact, rumor has it that he donates all his consulting money to charity efforts abroad."

"Did he seem happier?" Phil asked.

"Yes and no. He seemed more satisfied after his trips, although sometimes he would be cold and impatient!"

"How so?" Phil persisted.

"Well, I went to him with a personal problem last fall. He reacted strangely. 'Get a life,' he told me, 'I don't have time for your petty problems.' He didn't allow me to explain at all. The next day, though, he apologized. A few days later he was back to his normal self." Laura shrugged her shoulders.

"Maybe he framed his problem in a different way," Phil volunteered.

Laura smiled slightly and asked, "Why do we *always* use our classroom jargon in our regular conversations? What will it take to talk like normal people?"

"A brain lobotomy might do the trick," Phil grinned. "Perhaps it's the campus atmosphere. Maybe we're locked in our classroom frame. See, I can't get out of my frame!" He pressed his hands in front of himself like a mime trying to break out of a glass cage.

"There's a simple explanation," Laura interjected.

"What?" Phil was still pretending to get out of the glass frame.

"We aren't normal. We're a bunch of nerds, competing for the title of the chief nerd in town!" Laura laughed.

"Laura, can I ask you for a favor?" I said.

"Sure, Larry, what is it?"

"Can I borrow your laptop for a few days?"

"Sure—provided you buy dinner."

Laura was still laughing as she handed her computer to me. I glanced at the students sitting at the adjoining table. Paul Gerber caught my attention. He was examining Laura as he listened to the others talking around him. He curled his lips tightly. I couldn't fathom if he was smiling or grimacing. Laura noticed Paul's glances, and she abruptly stopped laughing.

"Let's go," Laura stood up to bus her tray.

* * *

Phil, Laura, and I were coming out of Billy's on Rush Street at 11:00 on Thursday night. We had a few beers under our belts. A light fog had descended low on the streets. Curls of vapor circled up in the cold air when we talked.

"Are you sure you want to drive?" Laura asked Phil. "We can always call for a taxi."

Phil took out his car keys. "I had two beers in the last four hours, nothing in the last two. I'm fine. Ask me a tough question."

"What's an accountant without a personality?" Laura teased.

"A boring accountant who's in the red?"

"No! An economist!" Laura laughed at her own joke, emitting ripples of light cascading music.

Phil grinned as he drove. We headed down a one-way residential street where the speed limit was forty miles per hour—Phil was going at thirty-five. Cars were parked on both sides of the narrow street.

Laura posed another riddle. "How many supply-side economists does it take to screw in a light bulb?"

"Three, one to do it, and two to hold him," I volunteered.

"None. They're waiting for the invisible hand to do it for them!" Laura's burst of cascading laughter filled the car.

Suddenly, a flashing image of a dress appeared on the windshield. Phil slammed on the brakes. We heard a sickening thud.

"My God! I hit somebody!" Phil screamed as he scrambled out of the car.

The crumpled figure of a young girl came into focus. She had been hit by the edge of the car and flung to the curbside. All three of us were at her side in an instant. Her right ankle was twisted inwards, a sure sign of a broken bone. She was unconscious and her breathing was shallow.

Phil called 911 on his cell phone: "Get an ambulance right away. We have a serious accident, close to the intersection of Fullerton and Clark Street." His voice trembled. Laura laid her jacket over the girl to keep her warm.

A middle-aged man came out from the house across the street.

"Mary Ellen, where are you?"

He saw the car and his girl. "Jesus! What have you done to my kid?" he yelled as he ran over to us.

"I'm sorry! The cars parked on both sides of the street blocked our vision," I tried to explain. "She darted in front of our car and we couldn't stop. She seems to have broken her foot. An ambulance is on the way."

The man was beside himself. "You bastards!" he fumed, as he knelt to examine his daughter. Meanwhile, a cop car had pulled up.

"Officer, my name is Phillip Myers. I'm a detective at Precinct 9. I was driving the car. I had two beers in the last four hours.

Give me a breathalyzer test right away!" Phil spoke rapidly, but the tremor in his voice was more controlled.

The cop assessed the situation, "You called 911. You don't have to take a breathalyzer test. I can double check your reflexes."

"Give him the breathalyzer test, damn it," the man yelled at the cop. "He hurt my daughter!"

Phil sighed, "I waive all my rights. Give me the breathalyzer test now!"

* * *

The ER waiting room had a rhythm of its own. In the last twenty minutes, three accident cases had been wheeled into examination rooms all at once. Now there was an eerie sense of tranquility. The only sound was an occasional announcement over the intercom, paging a doctor or a nurse. Phil, Laura, and I sat in the far corner of the waiting room. Mary Ellen had been wheeled in almost an hour ago. Phil held his head in his hands.

"Trust me to screw everything up. I shouldn't have driven the car. A cop driving drunk! I hope they do something about this," he fumed.

"Phil, your blood alcohol concentration was 0.02 percent— well below the legal limit. You shouldn't have driven the car, that's true. But she ran in front of the car suddenly and there was no time to react. The same thing could have happened if I was driving," I tried to assess the situation objectively.

"Tell that to the father. Besides, alcohol stays in your system for a long time. If I'd reacted a fraction of a second sooner, it could have made all the difference. My reflexes were impaired. I can't blame anyone except myself!"

"What was a young girl doing in the street at 11:00 on a week night?" I asked.

"Why does that matter?"

We later learned she had been celebrating a late birthday party. She was going across the street to say goodnight to her grandmother.

Laura joined in, "Mary Ellen has a multiple fracture in the ankle. The way she was flung from the car, I feared much worse. The doctors say that she'll need two pins. She'll be fine in the long run."

"Tell that to the mother," Phil said. "There's no doubt that I've messed things up real bad. I need to speak to Mary Ellen's parents."

Phil stood up and walked slowly toward the hospital ward, his feet dragging on the carpet floor. I had to figure out a way to comfort him. Little did I know that the traffic accident with Mary Ellen would cast a long dark shadow—a shadow that would stretch over several years....

5
Weigh the Anchor without Rancor

The only person who behaves sensibly is my tailor.
He takes my measures anew every time he sees me.
All the rest go on with their old measurements.
—George Bernard Shaw

I had an inkling of what was going on in Phil's mind. He had a refined sense of fair play and justice. He could not condone his decision to drive the car with some alcohol in his system, and he was punishing himself. I called him in the morning.

"Phil, you okay?"

"I talked to Shawn Douglas last night," he answered. "I want him to put a note about the traffic accident in my official file. My insurance will pay all the medical costs. I have also asked Shawn to withdraw twenty-thousand dollars from my pension fund for Mary Ellen. I don't think I can undo what has happened, Larry. I'll pay for this every day!"

"You're overreacting, Phil. I was talking to Laura about this accident. She went through a rough time when her sister Diane was murdered. Laura blamed herself for not protecting Diane. Whenever the results turn out badly, we blame ourselves for making a wrong decision. It's called *post-decision regret*, and it's normal. Your feelings are more intense because someone else is bearing the consequences of your decision. You keep blaming yourself for deciding to drive last night. But almost any decision can have bad consequences. Things could have worked out the same regardless of your decision."

"That's a cop out! We have to take responsibility for our mistakes, don't we?" The anguish in Phil's voice was palpable.

"Yes—if you make a mistake, you have to take responsibility and learn from it. Laura's instincts made a choice for her in a split second. She can't rewind the clock and do it again to see if another choice would have worked out better. I guess she'll never know if fighting the murderer would have been better than running away. We have to try to make the best decision, but once we've made the decision, we can't continue to blame ourselves if there's a bad outcome."

"Larry, I didn't make the right decision. I shouldn't have driven the car. You know it, I know it. Don't sugarcoat my mistake. I have to take responsibility. I don't know how I'll make this situation any better."

"You sound like Lord Jim in Joseph Conrad's novel. Jim deserted his ship at a critical juncture, and the guilt about his cowardice nagged him continuously. So he tried to find a way to redeem himself. Eventually, he offered his life as a down payment for a peace agreement between two warring tribes. When the armistice broke, he forfeited his life as he'd promised. Before he died to fulfill his promise, he experienced a peculiar sense of contentment. He had confronted his demons and had proven to himself that he was not a coward. Some amount of guilt is natural, Phil, but you don't want to be like Jim. In any case, you want to avoid *hypervigilance.*"

"Hyper- what?"

"Hypervigilance. It's a condition of high emotional stress and arousal that's caused when we perceive imminent danger. For instance, a person in a burning house might run around aimlessly without trying to find the stairwell. When the mind is hypervigilant, our actions become frantic and our cognitive functions are compromised. On second thought, I used the wrong word. I don't think you're anywhere close to hypervigilant. You're still functioning normally. You probably have an acute form of post-decision regret. At some level you want to punish yourself for making the wrong decision. In Lord Jim's case, the post-decision regret caused him his life."

"Can you do me a favor?"

"Sure. What is it?"

"Please don't bring up the traffic accident again. Don't get me wrong. I appreciate your advice. Talking with you has helped, but I have to sort out my own problem. *Lord Jim* sounds like a rousing story, but I'm not that noble. You won't find me making peace between two warring tribes. I'll just stew in my own guilt!"

"I won't bring it up again, Phil. I hope to see you in class today. Just be gentle with yourself, won't you?"

* * *

Laura and I walked to the library for a discussion with our frame team. I noticed that something was still bothering her. After some coaxing she confessed.

"I think I have a problem with Paul Gerber."

"What kind of a problem?"

"Well, Paul has asked me out several times even though he knows that I'm in a relationship with you. Every time I've tried to make an excuse—hoping that he'll get the message. The last two occasions have been very uncomfortable. He seems to resent the fact that I haven't jumped at the chance. You know what Paul was boasting about recently?"

"What?"

"When I was talking with Clara, Paul interrupted and tried to impress us. He hinted that he belonged to an exclusive chemistry club that has an underground network. He kept talking about why he belongs to this organization. Something to do with all kinds of lethal chemicals and euthanasia. Clara and I ignored his bragging, but he thought we were impressed. He just wouldn't stop. The whole thing was so weird."

I was stumped by this revelation. Paul didn't have a shortage of dates. In fact, he was known in the school as a ladies' man. Paul Gerber had a striking appearance. His face had a clean-cut symmetry. The refined nose, the clear blue eyes, and a six-foot, thin frame completed the impression that he had come down from Mount Olympus. But his temper was another matter. When he got angry, the rage fed an already smoldering volcano. Any small incident could spark an eruption. I remembered what he had done to the chair in the Commons. That incident had been referred to the discipline board. I could see why Laura was concerned about Paul.

"I can talk to Paul Gerber."

Laura hesitated for a second and then said, "No, I don't want you to do that, Larry."

"Why not? I think I can defuse the situation with Paul, but only if you'll let me."

"It might make the problem worse. My father taught me one thing, Larry, how to survive on my own. I realize you want to help, but I really don't need your help on this one. Trust me." Laura reached out and gently held my hand.

I searched Laura's face for any clues. Her bright, hazel eyes had softened, but their misty depth seemed impenetrable. The very space that enveloped us and embraced us now seemed to create a barrier between us. I had to find a way to reach out to her. I tried a different angle.

"Laura, I know you've been going through a rough time since Diane's murder. It would be difficult for anyone in your situation. Sometimes it helps to talk things out. You've helped me so much with my personal problems. Is there any way I can help you? Do you want to talk about it?"

"Sure, Larry. But there's not much to talk about. You know I have been taking Prozac® to cope with the tragedy. I don't think pills are necessary though, I feel fine."

"Before you stop taking your medicine, make sure you talk to your doctor. It's not a good idea to stop taking Prozac abruptly. It's probably better to phase it out slowly—under the doctor's supervision."

"I'll talk to the doctor. Don't worry, I am fine." Laura was distracted as she searched for something in her purse. "Now is not a good time to talk about all this."

"All right, Laura. Can we discuss it some time over the weekend?"

"Fine," Laura said, still rummaging through her purse. "Let's talk about it later."

I was concerned about Paul's odd behavior. But it was not clear what I could do at this point. To be candid, in a way, I was relieved Laura had declined my offer to talk to Paul. Maybe the best thing was to avoid a confrontation.

* * *

Laura, Phil, and I looked over Clara's shoulders as she downloaded information about Cicor from the Internet.

Clara turned to face us. "When we're investigating what happened at PACE, I don't think we should assume that the executives at PACE *always* made optimal decisions. I'm not saying that they didn't *try* to make correct decisions. But in spite of their best intentions, the executives at PACE could be subject to biases and prejudices—you know, sub-optimal behaviors."

"What do you have in mind, Clara?" Laura asked.

"I don't know for sure. Maybe we need to distinguish what PACE should have done from what they actually did. After all, to err is human, and organizations can succumb to many biases. What about *groupthink* behavior?"

Groupthink is a mindset that is sometimes found in a cohesive group that shares common illusions. It develops when individuals actively discourage self-criticism and indulge in collective rationalization. A misplaced sense of superiority tends to form within the group. Opponents or competitors are stereotyped, their capabilities are underestimated, and their limitations are exaggerated. Individuals magnify each other's misperceptions in a groupthink environment.

In a competitive economic environment, like-minded executives of a cohesive group may inadvertently cultivate a false sense of invulnerability. They may exaggerate the benefits of their product and highlight minor deficiencies of their competitor's product. One factor driving groupthink behavior is the social approval of the peers in the group. Members of the group hesitate to criticize because they want to be regarded as team players. Consciously or sub-consciously, they help fortify the shared illusions of the group. In order to avoid groupthink, it is important for any organization to encourage diversity of backgrounds and welcome different points of view. Loyalty should not be confused with constructive criticism.

Laura shook her head. "PACE's behavior doesn't conform to a groupthink stereotype. A classic example of groupthink is the decision-making process in President Kennedy's inner circle that led to the Bay of Pigs fiasco. The Kennedy administration embarked on a foolhardy mission to invade Cuba. Administration officials stifled criticism, developed an illusion of invulnerability, and grossly underestimated the Cuban forces. It is possible PACE didn't encourage adequate criticism during its decision-making process. Corporate executives could have had a false impression about their competitors. But this wasn't typical groupthink behavior as in the Bay of Pigs."

Clara peered at the computer screen. "I guess Laura is right—this is not a regular pattern of groupthink behavior. After all, when PACE conducts medical trials under the supervision of the FDA, they have to abide by rigorous standards. These external benchmarks are likely to prevent groupthink behavior. What about other kinds of biases?"

Laura looked at her class notes. "What about *anchoring*? Professor Armstrong asked us to think about reference points. We know that most people latch on to anchors or reference points to simplify their thinking. These anchors may or may not be arbitrary. In fact, research demonstrates that people often cling to irrelevant anchors. Even when they are told that the anchors are complete nonsense, they still use them."

"What kind of anchor are we talking about?" Clara asked.

"It could be any type of reference point," Laura replied. "Here's a common example: Most sales can be regarded as a 'three by two' operation. Multiply the initial wholesale cost by three to obtain the retail price. The retail price becomes an anchor, and we predicate our thinking based on this price. Stores divide the retail price by two to offer a sale discount. Don't we often congratulate ourselves? I got a good deal, 50 or 70 percent off the retail price! But on what basis was the retail price set? If the retail price was arbitrary, the discount has no meaning."

I knew what Laura was talking about. Who hasn't anchored their thoughts to an arbitrary reference point? I was once stuck with a bad stock of a high-tech company. The price kept going downhill. I kept waiting for the price to go up so that I could sell the stock for close to what I had paid for it. My buying price had become a psychological anchor. The relevant question: Would I buy the stock now at the existing low price? If the answer was no, I should have dumped it.

Laura walked over to pick up a computer printout. Paul Gerber leaned across and smiled as he talked to Laura. I could sense Laura's body tense up. Her shoulder blades arched noticeably higher. As Paul finished his conversation, he wasn't smiling any more. The whole encounter lasted a few minutes. When Laura came back to our group, she seemed visibly disturbed. I wanted to talk to her about Paul, but Clara asked a question.

"I guess the context of the reference point is also important, don't you think?"

"Yes, the context changes our interpretation of the reference point," I said allowing Laura some time to collect herself. "A good performance, during an economic expansion, could be a sales growth of 12 percent. During a recession, a sales threshold of 5 percent can be regarded as quite good. We don't want our thinking to be confounded by irrelevant or inappropriate anchors. Remember Professor Armstrong's mantra: *Weigh the anchor without rancor.*"

"What does he mean by 'weigh' the anchor?" Clara asked.

Laura had regained her composure. She jumped in: "By *weighing,* Professor Armstrong meant that we need to recognize how an anchor influences our thinking. We need to ignore an anchor if it is arbitrary, but we can also use it to our advantage. An anchor can be employed as an effective tool in negotiation or bargaining. If you want the sales commission to be set at 8 percent, start by making a strong case for 11 percent. Ultimately, when you drop down to 8 percent, it will appear as if you've given up a lot. You have to justify the anchor of 11 percent though so that the compromise doesn't appear to be a setup."

I noticed Laura was talking intensely. In times of deep concentration, her forehead would crinkle up—I just loved the shape of her crinkles. She was not standing in her normal relaxed posture. The tension with Paul Gerber was probably getting to her. Laura had taught me about how to open up to her—now she seemed to be closing up. I had a sense of déjà vu. My mother had withdrawn to an inner world, and my attempts to draw her out had failed. I did not want to repeat the pattern with Laura. Maybe I was overreacting. I was glad she had agreed to talk about it over the weekend.

Clara said, "All this information about anchoring is good, but was PACE clinging to some anchors? Were the anchors arbitrary?"

Laura flipped another page of her class notes. "Let's see . . . PACE was trying to develop a medicine that would dramatically reduce cholesterol. One potential anchor is the performance standard set by existing statin drugs. For instance, a landmark study demonstrated that a statin called Pravastatin—marketed under the brand name Pravachol®—reduced total cholesterol levels by 20 percent. The 20 percent reduction may have been an anchor for PACE. The company was trying to provide a product that would reduce cholesterol by much more than 20 percent."

I brought up another possibility: "Donald was talking about the amount of money PACE is planning to spend on finding new therapies. PACE has spent fifteen billion dollars on heart-related research. The company has to make a profit like everyone else. Isn't it possible for this investment to become an anchor? Rather than take a long-term view, PACE may be trying to recover the fifteen billion dollars too quickly."

Clara pointed to the computer screen. "I didn't find anything in here to indicate that PACE executives relied on arbitrary anchors. The thresholds we just talked about could be used as anchors, but we're only guessing. Most of those anchors can be justified as reasonable guideposts. If PACE executives became too obsessed with a specific reference point, it could distort their thinking, but we don't know for sure whether that took place."

I glanced at Phil. He appeared to be listening, but his eyes told a different story. Their glazed look indicated that his mind was elsewhere. He had said nothing during the discussion. *If only I could distract his attention in some way and get him out of his guilt trip. I should think of something to do with both Laura and Phil over the weekend. Going to a concert or a play might be good therapy for both of them.*

Clara collected her books as she continued: "One thing is becoming clear—the frame is enlarged as we actively question our presumptions and look at the issue from different viewpoints. If we look at it from PACE's point of view, we get one picture. If we consider it from the perspective of the doctors, patients, or the FDA, we get other takes on the same picture. I guess this mystery is not going to have a simple solution. I'll ask Stewart Anderson and some other students to join us next week. Maybe we can dig up information about the role played by doctors and patients."

My stomach was making grumbling noises. It was time for a break.

* * *

As Laura and I left for lunch, she reached out and held my hand. "Larry, about the discussion we were planning to have over the weekend, can we do it some other time? I need to catch up on a bunch of chores." She pressed my hand gently.

I sensed Laura was withdrawing. Perhaps an indirect approach might work better.

"How about going to a concert tonight? You can do your chores on Saturday and Sunday. A diversion will do us both some good."

Laura nodded. "That's a great idea. Let's see if Clara or Phil are interested."

Was Laura trying to include others so that we couldn't discuss any personal matters? She had never before tried to avoid a frank discussion with me. I was bothered by her cryptic behavior, but I did not want to dwell on it. Maybe the best thing to do was to call her over the weekend when she was more relaxed.

"Sounds good! Let's plan on a concert in the evening," I replied.

Phil Meyers and Paul Gerber joined us at the lunch table. As Paul sat down, Laura said, "Hey, Paul! The e-mail you sent about the new psychological biases was very interesting. Thanks a lot."

Paul grunted. "The e-mail wasn't more interesting than you!" he said, looking directly at her. Laura's face flushed slightly. I broke the uncomfortable silence. "Hey, guys! Thank God it's Friday! Who wants to go to the blues concert in Grant Park?"

No one responded. I glanced at Paul. His right hand grasped the edge of the table. His knuckles were white from the exertion.

I stood up in mock disbelief, "No one likes the blues?"

Phil sighed, "I'm not a blues fan. I guess I'll tag along if you guys are going."

I was hoping my friendly overture would diffuse some of the tension with Paul, but he gathered his books without another word. He completely ignored my invitation.

The blues concert on Friday night was a blast. Both Laura and Phil appeared to have a good time. The concert put us all in a better mood. The weekend drifted by quickly. I tried to catch up on my reading and complete pending chores.

I am not a morning person. On Monday morning, I was sound asleep in my room at 8:00, when a sharp rap on the door awakened me. Then the rapping turned into pounding. I woke up in a stupor and stumbled toward the door.

"Who is it?" I muttered. "Can't you use the doorbell?"

I opened the door and saw Phil. He was breathing hard. His face was ashen. He hunched his shoulders and came into the room. His voice had a slight quiver as he spoke. "Something awful has happened! You better sit down."

6
Cause and Effect Is Hard to Detect

Domestic animals expect food when they see the person who feeds them.
The man who has fed the chicken every day
throughout its life at last wrings its neck instead!

—Bertrand Russell
(On why the same sequence
doesn't imply cause and effect)

I saw Phil's lips moving. I heard the words. The words were simple enough—Laura was dead! I was stunned. All I could think was that my life will never be the same. I heard the details as if caught in a slow-motion nightmare.

Clara had gone to Laura's campus apartment at 6:30 that morning to ask her to go to a demonstration. The door was unlocked, and Clara found Laura's body. It looked like suicide. She appeared to have injected herself with a massive chemical cocktail that contained sodium pentothal. Phil explained that sodium pentothal, if administered in a large dose, would stop the heart and lungs. As Phil talked, my mind went numb. I couldn't cry. A heavy lead ball sat in my stomach.

"Can we go to her room now?" I heard myself asking.

"The detective squad is in her room right now. Shawn Douglas and his men are working the room. Shawn called me as soon as he found out. It seems like suicide, but they want to check things out. Let's walk over together."

As I picked up my jacket, the lead ball in my stomach oozed acid. Outside, a chilly wind stung my face. It was welcome relief, but I thought, Laura will never feel this wind again.

In fifteen minutes we were outside Laura's room. There was no tape around the door, but a police detective was in the corridor. Phil nodded to him as we approached. "It's okay," he murmured. "We won't touch anything. I have asked Shawn's permission to look at the room."

As we walked in, I saw Laura. She was slumped over the table, her shoulders resting on the tabletop. Her right hand was hanging down, her fingers almost touching the floor. A hypodermic needle was on the floor near her right hand. She was wearing a bright yellow sweater and jeans; her hair was rumpled. She had a peaceful expression on her face, as if after a long study session, she had fallen asleep at the table!

I looked around the room. There was no sign of a struggle. Everything was neatly arranged as usual. Laura always kept a tidy apartment. The closet doors were wide open. Her clothes were neatly arranged with her shoes and boots lined up. Next to the shoes lay a neatly folded, brown electric blanket. I thought, that's odd. Why would she place the electric blanket next to the shoes? Phil interrupted my thoughts.

"There's no sign of a break-in. Shawn left a few minutes ago. I'll ask him if they found anything else. Professor Armstrong and Donald have been informed. Do you want to stay here?"

I looked at Laura's limp body. A cold pulsating sensation vibrated through my body and settled on the base of my spine.

"No. But can I go with her when they move her body?"

Phil nodded, "I'll arrange it. I think they'll be moving her to the funeral home pretty soon."

* * *

There was no class on Monday. Grief strikes people in different ways. Phil Myers became more talkative. Professor Armstrong wore a somber expression. Paul Gerber holed up in his room. Raj Kumar increased his meditation sessions. Clara was unable to talk to anybody. She went to the library and read continuously. Donald fired two more employees. Stewart Anderson talked more intensely with his laptop. John Scott dropped his voice to a permanent whisper. Several classmates tried to console each other. I tried to neutralize my stomach acid by taking huge gulps of Mylanta®.

Phil came to my room in the evening. Now that he was focused on Laura's death, his mind was no longer on his car accident. He kept talking—trying to establish normalcy through conversation. I didn't want to talk at all, but having Phil around was comforting.

"Shawn Douglas and his crew believe that Laura committed suicide," he said. "They found extra doses of Prozac in her apartment. The prescription was filled three months ago, but almost all the pills are still there. She hadn't taken her pills for several weeks."

A pang of guilt swept over me. I had seen signs that something was amiss, but hadn't adequately followed up. I could have prevented the suicide. Phil shifted to a more mundane topic. "Do you believe it? We're having class tomorrow in Cook County Hospital. Professor Armstrong should cancel class for a week."

I was going over each recent meeting with Laura. On Friday, she told me she had to catch up with several things over the weekend. I should have insisted on meeting her on Saturday or Sunday. I had planned to call her on Saturday, but never got around to it. Instead, I had spent the time performing meaningless chores and catching up on my reading. Perhaps subconsciously I was trying to avoid a confrontation with her. What if I had insisted that she visit the campus counseling center? What if I had asked Professor Armstrong for his help? Why couldn't I have seen it coming? Maybe I didn't know Laura as well as I thought. The lead ball in my stomach had splintered into sharp fiery pieces. Meanwhile, Phil had returned to the investigation.

"I'm not sure you want to hear this right now. We need to talk about Laura's death. Can I ask you some questions?"

I needed some time alone to absorb the emotional shock. I reached for my Mylanta bottle again. "Ask me tomorrow. Right now, I have to call my brother. After that, I want to crawl under my blanket and try to sleep."

Chris looks at me with concern.

"Larry, are you all right? I can tell from your voice that you still feel the pain, don't you?"

"No, Chris, it usually doesn't hurt anymore. Time has altered things. The constant dull ache has gone. Rarely, in a flash, it comes back, but the

anguish has found a new language. Sometimes, many times, an old wound speaks to me, and I hear Laura's voice whisper."

"What do you mean?"

"The flashes of intense hurt are infrequent and different now. At first, I fought these episodes. The pain would return in different disguises: sometimes, like an old tumor that encroaches on different parts of the mind—many times, as a listless spirit that refuses to soar. After almost a year, I learned how to deal with my demons. I welcomed them and tried to feel the pain as much as I could. As I opened myself up to the loss and anguish, over time, I healed. Now, when Laura speaks infrequently, it's not painful anymore. It's mostly nostalgia and what could have been."

"I'm not sure I get what you're telling me, Larry. Did you cry that night, after Laura died?"

"For many nights I would lie in bed with an overwhelming desire to cry. My face would contort, but tears wouldn't come. Somehow, the healing power of tears hasn't been part of my nature. I'm trying to be honest about all this, Chris, because I want you to be in touch with your emotions. I haven't seen you cry since you were ten years old. If you can do it, crying is good therapy. Either way, you have to accept the pain and grieve for some time. If you run away from it or try to push it down, it'll probably return in a more virulent form."

"You called me that night, didn't you?"

"Yes, I did, while I was gulping down the Mylanta©."

"But you never mentioned Laura's death. Why didn't you share one of your worst nights with me?"

"I rationalized that you were already stressed out with what was happening with Mom. The real reason was that at that time I didn't even know how to grieve, let alone share the pain with you. It all happened so fast. As I get older, I have been recollecting those days and trying to imbibe more of the insights. Information is easy to get—we can download almost everything from the Internet with a click of a mouse. What we do with the information—the awareness to open our minds and the wisdom to temper our spirits—takes more than a lifetime. As you reflect on this information over time, it will make more and more sense to you. Remember information is easy to get, we need awareness to gain more knowledge, but wisdom…often lingers."

"Okay, Larry, I won't press the delete button—I'll store this data in a cache somewhere. But go on with the story. What happened after that?"

"Well, the next day a different world awaited me. A world without Laura...."

* * *

Cook County Hospital was the last place I felt like going Tuesday morning. My stomach was still on fire. Sitting in my room and brooding the whole day was not a good alternative either. As I entered the hospital lobby the smell of iodine crept into my nostrils. I made my way to the conference room on the second floor.

Raj Kumar was introducing his brother, Dr. Sunder Kumar, to the class. "My frame team is examining the Cicor case from the medical point of view. I have asked my brother, Dr. Sunder Kumar, to contribute to this discussion. We will be talking about tracing cause and effect. First, though, I would like to say a few words about Laura...." As Raj began, his eyes traveled to Professor Armstrong and then settled on me.

"We will miss Laura—no doubt about it. I know our thoughts are about her today, as we try to cope with the tragedy. In this hospital, as in any other hospital, births and deaths occur every day. Yet, for the living, time moves on. We will carry this loss with us forever—some more than others." He looked directly at me. "Let us always remember her grace and warmth...." At this point, Raj was at a loss for words.

Professor Armstrong sighed, "Thank you for the kind words, Raj. One way to try to handle our grief is to transfer our attention to the matter at hand. Let's get the discussion rolling."

There was a strained silence as Raj began in a hesitant voice: "Immanuel Kant, the German philosopher, believed that human reason perceives almost everything as a matter of cause and effect. Kant thought that looking for cause and effect was an intrinsic human attribute. It is easy to think that one thing causes another, but it is almost impossible to prove it beyond any doubt. I propose a new mantra: Cause and effect is hard to detect."

Raj's voice grew stronger. "Let us start with an example. Does eating food high in saturated fats cause heart disease? We know that people who eat large amounts of saturated fats frequently develop heart disease more often than those who follow a low-fat diet. This association could be because those who have a bad diet also do not exercise enough, or drink too much, or are obese. Any of these confounding factors can result in an association between a bad diet and heart disease. The important issue is, holding everything else constant, to what extent do saturated fats cause heart disease?"

Professor Armstrong joined in: "Raj makes an important point: Confounding factors confound. Most scientific experiments are judged by how well we control for these confounding factors. Have we correctly accounted for other variables that could result in an association between the two factors we are observing? In the case of saturated fats and heart disease, what other elements are missing?"

Raj Kumar's darting eyes settled on Professor Armstrong. "Several things. It could be that our results are due to some other factor unique to the group. For instance, some cultures eat more fish, which may prevent heart disease. To examine the relationship between saturated fats and heart disease, we have to assemble a group of individuals who are similar to the population at large. We have to ensure that different races, ages, and income levels of both men and women are represented in our group. Even if we have a representative sample, the result could still have an element of chance. This means that the investigation will have to be corroborated by other studies applying different controls."

Phil entered the conference room. He appeared tired, but his eyes glistened with anticipation. Raj shifted gears, "Dr. Sunder Kumar will explain how medical studies try to pin down whether Cicor was effective therapy for patients. Remember PACE had to demonstrate the safety and efficacy of the new medicine in experimental trials supervised by the FDA. We will discuss how the protocol established by the FDA attempts to associate cause and effect."

Dr. Kumar stepped forward. He adjusted his glasses and rubbed his hands, as if scrubbing before surgery. His voice was deep and throaty.

"PACE had to demonstrate the effectiveness and safety of Cicor by conducting many medical trials. A typical FDA trial would identify two representative groups of patients who are similar to patients at large. An experimental group is 'treated' by the new statin drug. The control group is given a dummy pill or placebo. We can investigate if the new medicine results in a demonstrable improvement for the patients in the treatment group compared to the effect of the placebo in the control group."

Phil nudged my arm from the back as he passed me a note: *Are you ready to talk about Laura after class?* I turned around and nodded.

Dr. Kumar continued: "It is important to set up the experiment in this manner because of the placebo effect. Persons who take a dummy pill *might think* they are feeling better and the positive feeling could reduce their symptoms. Some studies show that the placebo effect could influence 30 percent of the control group. Other chance factors can also affect the results. We need to measure a substantial improvement among the patients in the treatment group who are taking Cicor, *over and above the effect demonstrated by the placebo in the control group.*"

"What about the side effects of the new medicine?" Clara asked. "We need to worry about the safety of Cicor, don't we?"

"I should point out that safety and side effects are also analyzed by comparing the patients of the control group with the patients of the treatment group. People complain about many kinds of health problems all the time—sore backs, headaches, and nausea. These normal complaints will routinely occur in both the treatment and control groups. The issue becomes whether the side effects in the treatment group are indeed substantially higher compared to the placebo group."

Clara persisted: "We're making a critical assumption that the patients in the treatment and control groups accurately represent all patients at large. My research shows that many of the patients who died while taking Cicor had many other complications. In contrast, the patients in the treatment and control groups were generally healthier. Moreover, only male patients participated in the study. The average older patient at large is generally less healthy and is taking two other prescription drugs. Consequently, the actual risk of complications for Cicor patients could be higher than what is indicated by the experimental trials. Wouldn't you agree?"

Dr. Kumar rubbed his hands again. "You have a good point. If the patients in the treatment and control groups are not representative of the average patient at large, we have a serious problem. The results about the safety and efficacy of Cicor demonstrated in the experimental trials may be misleading."

Phil passed another note to me: *Let's slip out of class.* I shook my head slightly. Listening to the class discussion was keeping my mind off Laura, at least for a short while. As I tried to focus on the class discussion, I noticed that Paul Gerber seemed restless. His eyes drifted back and forth, as if looking for something. I couldn't detect any emotion on his face.

Raj picked up the discussion: "It is clear from this conversation that there are several possibilities as far as cause and effect are concerned. Take another example: from an entirely different area—crime, for instance. Does a lack of education really increase crime rates? Let us assume we find an association between lower education levels and higher crime rates. There are actually five possibilities. Can anyone explain some of the possibilities?"

John Scott replied, "First, lower education—that is more high school dropouts with no skills—could increase crime. Second, persons who commit more crime may end up in jail and spend less time on education—higher crime could lead to less education. Third, both the first and second possibility could coexist. Lower education and higher crime might cause each other."

Raj nodded, "Those are three possibilities John, and here are two more. Lower education and higher crime rates might be linked by a confounding factor, such as higher poverty or a larger proportion of younger persons who tend to commit more crimes. Finally, lower education and higher crime rates might be correlated by mere chance. In order to focus on the net effect of lower education on high crime rates, we have to account for the other four possibilities."

I looked around the conference room. I could not stop thinking about Laura. Her bright, energetic face kept creeping into my mind. Where would Laura be sitting right now if she were here? Maybe she would sit next to Stewart as he cajoled his laptop. No, she would probably sit next to Clara.

Laura had a unique capacity to make many close friends. As we became good friends, she had showed me a part of myself that I did not know existed. The strife between my parents and the tribulations of my mother had bruised my emotions. Without knowing it, I had started to become a robot—all action and no emotional depth.

Laura taught me how to rediscover and embrace my feelings. I picked up my cues from how she related to me. She would try to understand where I was coming from, to validate my emotions and my thinking. As we grew closer, she taught me how to love in a new way—to love the whole person. I learned how we could understand each other's faults and get past them. Her lessons were powerful because she modeled them. She tempered my youthful passion with a spiritual dimension. Laura encouraged me to start my inward journey—to try to find a space within me that I could retreat to as a safe harbor. "Find your true self, Larry," she would say, "before you find me."

The irony of her words was hard to bear. She was right next to me and I had lost her. I had been caught up in trying to find myself—in building my own romantic notions— living in my own fantasy world. She had given me so many different signs that she needed my help. But I was too self-absorbed—too caught up in my own bubble of romantic energy—I had failed to respond to her actual needs. Now she was gone. The small, fiery pieces in my stomach were somersaulting. Sharp pinprick sensations nibbled my insides.

I tried to focus on Professor Armstrong's voice. "Raj's example illustrates the difficulty of establishing cause and effect. Do you have anything else to say, Raj?"

Raj Kumar had a whimsical look. "I want to bring up a different type of cause and effect. The ancient Hindu philosophers may not have understood the intricacies of setting up an experiment— but they knew it is almost impossible to trace cause and effect relationships in one's lifetime, let alone across births. So the central idea of Karma was born."

John Scott was all ears: "I didn't know Karma had to do with cause and effect. What's the central idea of Karma?"

Raj looked at Dr. Kumar. "I am sure my brother would agree that the notion of Karma is widely misunderstood. The central idea is that at each point of our life we can never *really know* what is good or bad for us. That does not mean that we should not try to do what we think is right. Doing the right thing creates positive energy by linking other causes and effects with it."

"Does Karma mean we should resign ourselves to our fate?" John asked.

Raj shook his head, "No, it does not mean that we should stop trying. Why eliminate a causal link? However, having tried our best, let it go! We should not pile on the stress by second guessing ourselves all the time. Both good and bad actions can have unintended and unpredictable consequences. We really don't know for sure if an action that we think is right will have positive or negative results in the end. In an ultimate sense, we have to give ourselves up to the cosmic force, or whatever we think is out there."

How could I let Laura go? I did not know how to give myself up to a cosmic force. I had to make some sense out of the tragedy. Some students were wondering how a discussion about cause and effect had slipped into the philosophy of Karma. There was a great deal of whispering going on at the back. Professor Armstrong appeared deep in thought. As the noise level increased, he raised his hands: "On this spiritual note, we'll adjourn until the next time."

Phil caught up with me as we left the conference room.

"Larry, some things don't add up in Laura's case. Shawn Douglas thinks it's a clear case of suicide. But I learned something unusual. Laura went to a travel agent on Saturday afternoon to make plans for a spring vacation."

"How did you get that information?" I couldn't keep the surprise out of my voice.

"You know how Professor Armstrong has been asking us to actively question our presumptions? He coined a word for it—be a *contrarian*. Try to look for information that is contrary to your beliefs. Police detectives often develop prior beliefs before all the evidence is collected. They subconsciously tend to look for facts that validate their prior hunches. They fall into what Professor Armstrong calls a 'confirmation bias.' Do you remember what I'm talking about?"

"Yes . . . Yes! I remember that discussion very well. But how did you find out about Laura's travel plans?"

"After I left your apartment last night, I went back to Laura's room. The police had long gone home. I asked Shawn if I could look over the room. He told me to be very careful and wear gloves. I knew the police were looking for the usual telltale signs of a struggle—fingerprints, blood, and broken or scattered things. I started going over Laura's desk. In the second drawer I noticed a brochure about Carnival Cruises®." Phil paused.

"Go on!"

"You know spring break is three weeks away. I started wondering—maybe she met a travel agent recently. The travel agency's phone number and address were stamped on the back of the brochure. I called the agency today before coming to class. Laura visited the travel agency at 3:00 p.m. on Saturday. Would you make travel plans on Saturday and then kill yourself on Sunday night?"

My head was spinning. "Depression can come in waves. It's possible that she had a sudden onset on Sunday night."

"Possible but not likely," Phil interjected. "We need to check Laura's phone logs from last weekend. But first we need to meet our discussion group. Remember, we're supposed to meet Clara and the others at the library. We should at least go to the meeting and talk to them, don't you think?"

I noticed that the small, fiery pieces in my stomach were settling down. "I guess we should go and meet them. Maybe we can make an excuse and ask the group to meet some other time. I'd really like to get more information about Laura."

"While you're meeting with the group, I'll call the phone company from the library and try to trace the phone logs." Phil was already getting into his car.

7
Gravitate to Your Own Risk Taste

True luck consists not in holding the best cards at the table;
Luckiest is he who knows just when to rise and go home.
—John Hay

The library at St. Andrews was still called the library—not the "media center" as in some trendy places. St. Andrews had been voted as one of the best-wired campuses in the country, but most of the computers were tucked away unobtrusively in adjacent labs. The school had made it a point not to forsake the polished bookcases—and to preserve the joy of flipping through books. But most students clustered around in the computer labs. Cruising the Internet was the preferred way not only to acquire information but also to socialize.

Phil and I made our way to the computer lab in the far corner. As we passed by the main reading room, I saw two students furiously searching through a law journal. On the adjacent table, a student was taking a nap—all the students around him ignored the rhythmic sounds of his breathing. Every now and then he would emit a loud snore. It was business as usual in the library—the last refuge for catching up on your sleep if not your reading. Contrary to Professor Armstrong's advice, not everyone who went to the library was excited.

Phil slipped out to call the phone company while I joined the study group. They were already discussing the Cicor case. John Scott, Stewart Anderson, and Clara Starr were listening to Raj Kumar. "PACE is under constant pressure to beat the competition. Cicor is a powerful drug. Normally the recommended dose is five-tenths of a milligram. The FDA quite quickly approved a higher dose of one milligram. The higher dose provides greater benefits, but the risk of serious side effects also multiplies. Where does this race for stronger drugs stop? More is not always better, is it? PACE needs to slow down—you know—adopt a safer pace!"

"I agree that more is not always better," Clara said. "There's competitive pressure to bring the drugs to the market quickly, without fully understanding the long-term consequences of the higher dosages. Although the FDA tries to ensure that the relative risks and benefits are evaluated by controlled trials, in many cases, the risks are not monitored for an extended period. On the other hand, the benefits of the new therapies can't be denied to patients indefinitely. I think, though, it's better to err on the side of safety."

Clara and Raj had a good point. Pharmaceutical companies should ensure the safety of new medicines beyond a reasonable doubt. Otherwise aggressive marketing of new products, with limited knowledge of their long-term complications, can often result in unintended consequences. Fifty-two people had died while taking Cicor. Some of these deaths were probably due to other factors. But PACE was in a tough situation. The negative publicity was continuing to build up. PACE had no choice but to withdraw Cicor on its own.

Paul Gerber walked into the room. He completely ignored our group. As he passed by, I noticed the dark shadows under his eyes. He walked to the far side of the room and sat in front of a computer terminal. His movements were quick and jerky as he typed furiously on the keyboard. I wondered what was going on with him. I was tempted to walk over and look at his computer screen.

John Scott added a different perspective: "There's another factor we haven't considered in this discussion. All of us have different preferences for risk. The amount of risk we're willing to tolerate depends on our personality and circumstances. Studies have shown that when regulators impose additional safety precautions—such as seat belts or airbags—we sometimes compensate by taking risks in other ways. This type of offsetting behavior has been dubbed the 'compensation hypothesis'."

"Now you're using technical words to intimidate me again," Clara jested. "Explain in simple terms what you mean by *compensation hypothesis*."

"Compensating behavior is more common than you think," John lowered his voice. "We drive to school and work every day. Seat belt laws are an attempt to enforce safety. We can get a ticket if we're driving without a seat belt. Drivers feel safer when they fasten their seat belts. Most people are risk averse, so they're comfortable with the additional safety. But for some, the additional safety measures encourage risk taking in other ways. Some people compensate by driving faster or creeping past stop signs. They end up killing more people outside their car! Seat belts don't provide additional safety for all of us."

I had read an article about the effectiveness of safety caps on medicine bottles. The article pointed out that safety caps didn't significantly reduce accidental ingestion of dangerous medicine by children. Before safety caps came along, parents were very careful about keeping medicines out of a child's reach. When safety caps became available, parents compensated by becoming more careless. Kids often figured out how to open safety caps. The result: Safety caps did not provide a great deal of additional safety.

John Scott raised his voice abruptly. "Professor Armstrong has a slogan for us: Gravitate to your own risk taste. He emphasized that, consciously or subconsciously, we try to go back to the risk level that is within our comfort zone. It's difficult to improve safety when our underlying preference for risk ultimately governs our behavior. We tend to regress back to our personal comfort level of risk."

"Great!" Clara intervened. "I think I get the general drift about the compensation hypothesis. How does this relate to Cicor? Wait a minute, I see the connection! If patients are feeling safer because they are taking Cicor, which significantly reduces their cholesterol levels, they may take risks in other ways—eat more fatty foods or exercise less frequently. Is that it?"

John smiled. "Yes, the effect of any medicine might be compromised if patients reduce their compliance to other kinds of preventive behavior. Now look at it from a corporate point of view. PACE has to follow a rigorous protocol to demonstrate the safety of their medicines in the FDA trials. But the company may be induced to take risks in other ways; perhaps push for approval of higher dosages of Cicor without fully understanding the long-term consequences of the additional dosage. Taking more risk doesn't have to be deliberate—additional risk is often taken subconsciously."

Phil came back visibly disturbed. "Ameritech won't give any information over the phone," he whispered in my ear. "They want us to come to the corporate headquarters."

"Might as well go right now," I whispered back.

* * *

We were fortunate to find parking close to Ameritech's main office on Washington Street. As we entered the lobby area, I asked Phil, "What do you expect to find in the phone log?"

"We're going on a fishing expedition. Information about when and with whom she talked might be pertinent."

The manager of the records department at Ameritech was a tall, lanky person named Stan. He was waiting for Phil. Stan insisted on looking at Phil's identification before doing anything. Then he asked for Laura's phone number and the time frame of the calls. He went to his computer and typed some identifiers—phone number, days, and time. A log of all calls made from Laura's phone over the weekend appeared on the screen. Stan was scrolling down the list when Phil interrupted.

"Can I move the mouse?" he asked.

"Be my guest," Stan responded.

Phil slowly scanned the list for Friday and Saturday with the mouse. The list indicated the phone number called, the location of the phone number, the time, and the length of the call. There was nothing unusual for Friday and Saturday—except a call to the travel agency, probably to set up the appointment for Saturday afternoon. On Sunday, a phone call at 10:15 a.m. to a number in Boston had lasted for forty-five minutes!

"Do you recognize this number in Boston?" Phil asked.

I looked at the number with an 857 area code. "I can't be sure. This might be her friend Joan Hall who lives in Boston."

"Can you verify that, please?" Phil asked Stan. Within a few minutes it was confirmed that the number belonged to Joan. I had met Joan once when she had come to Chicago.

"Stan, can we call this number right now?" Phil looked at me. "Larry, do you want to talk to Joan?" I nodded.

Joan picked up the phone after two rings. I told her the bad news. She was, of course, shocked, hardly able to speak for several seconds.

"My God! I don't know what to say," gasped Joan. "I talked to Laura on Sunday morning. She seemed fine. We talked about our high school days. She told me that she was looking into some vacation plans. She was going to surprise you with a cruise, Larry."

I felt a sharp pain in my stomach. "Joan, did Laura seem depressed in any way when you spoke to her?"

Joan talked between sobs. "She seemed stressed out with all the school work. She was nostalgic about our high school days. There was a tinge of sadness in her voice, but she seemed in control. What do you think happened?"

"We don't know yet. We're trying to get more information. Thanks Joan, I'll call you later." I put down the phone.

Phil thanked Stan on the way out. "There isn't much more we can do here. Let's try to figure out our next step."

* * *

Chris is leaning forward in his chair, his elbows on his knees. Laura's death has made him sit up and listen intently.

"How could you try to get more information about Laura and keep going to classes and discussion groups at the same time? Didn't you feel like saying, 'Let's forget about school for a while. Let's just try to solve the case'?"

"I know it sounds weird—going to class and trying to solve the case at the same time. I think Phil and I realized that the decision-making class was somehow helping us—giving us new ways to bounce ideas and leads off each other. We didn't go to other classes—but Professor Armstrong's class provided a dynamic framework to discuss different aspects of the case."

Chris looks thoughtful. "I think I get most of the discussion about cause and effect. Kant was right—I tend to view and understand things as cause-and-effect relationships, but in many cases, the associations are more complex than we think, aren't they?"

"Yes. We need to realize that if two things are associated or correlated, cause and effect is only one possibility. We're inclined to think of causality as either existing or absent. The more interesting question is, "To **what degree** does one thing cause another?" We can easily attribute more to the cause-and-effect relationship than is warranted. For instance, to what extent does an increase in money supply result in lower interest rates? To measure the 'net' effect, we have to control for other factors that continuously influence interest rates: business conditions, the behavior of banks, and expected price changes, among others. Moreover, the reverse effect of interest rates on money supply and the role of random variation have to be evaluated."

Chris smiles as his mind drifts elsewhere. "What kind of risk preference do you have? I bet you're risk averse."

"Having lived with me, you know my risk preferences pretty well. There's enough uncertainty in life that we can't control. Why look for more trouble? The car is the most dangerous thing you touch everyday. Why speed up and risk everything you have? It's better to be safe than sorry. Young people appear to be risk takers, which is strange, as they potentially have more of their lives to lose. Perhaps they have a false sense of invulnerability because they don't perceive the dangers accurately or they don't process the facts objectively. There's no point in taking unnecessary risks, is there?"

"Sometimes it is a do-and-dare thing—to try to get the admiration of my friends. You don't have to worry about it, Larry. I think I know my limits. I wouldn't put myself in harm's way. Do you find yourself compensating when additional safety is imposed? I am not sure I get that."

"Those who prefer risk may react differently to additional safety regulations. They'll probably compensate by reducing their vigilance or taking risk in other ways. For the majority of us who are risk averse, additional safety is welcome. We may not compensate by increasing risk in other areas. Taking additional risk can be subtle. Subconsciously, my tolerance for risk can change. After wearing a seat belt, I might be less vigilant or go beyond the speed limit more frequently without fully realizing it."

Chris shifts to a different track. "What about the risks taken by executives of corporations such as Enron and WorldCom who made millions of dollars for themselves? They damaged their companies and were *unfair to shareholders. Don't tell me they are gravitating to their risk taste! Are you telling me we shouldn't penalize their behavior?"*

"Good point, Chris. We have to distinguish between legitimate risk taking and outrageous criminal conduct. It is hard to believe, as some of them claim, that they didn't know about the financial irregularities of their own companies. A more reasonable explanation is that most of them made a conscious decision to fudge their accounts and acquire immediate fortunes. The subsequent risk of being caught and paying fines appeared manageable to them. If you make several hundred million—a fine of a few million is peanuts. What they didn't expect was the stock market melt-down that forced lawmakers to enact more severe criminal punishments for this kind of behavior—I don't think going to prison was in their calculations."

"So what do we do with these guys?" Chris asks.

"Cooking the balance sheets for personal gain is a crime and anyone who's guilty should be prosecuted swiftly. But the fact still remains: We can't fine tune the amount of risk people will eventually take. We need to increase the transparency of balance sheets and ensure accountability by penalizing accounting fraud. Lack of accountability and information asymmetry are two major causes of market failure. However, some ex-ecutives will continue to take more risk than others. Indeed, a certain amount of differences in risk tastes is desirable—otherwise risky projects will never be undertaken. Fortunately, the financial markets are now sensitized to different kinds of accounting ambiguity. If companies don't improve the transparency of their balance sheets or hold their executives more accountable, their stock prices are punished more severely."

"Tell me what happened next."

"We tried to frame Laura's death the best way we could—we actively questioned our presumptions. Did Laura commit suicide or was she murdered? Obtaining more information, without raising suspicion was difficult. We didn't want anyone to start questioning what we were doing. Recalling past events accurately wasn't easy either. We were driving back from the Ameritech office—trying to reconstruct the past and deciding where we should look for more leads...."

8
Murder or Suicide? You Decide

To think is easy. To act is difficult.
To act as one thinks is the most difficult of all.
—Wolfgang Goethe

When we drove back from the Ameritech office, Phil was in a talkative mood.

"In the police academy, I had a teacher who trained us to look at a case from different angles. Make sure we ask probing questions. Consider all possible alternatives. I've found this strategy to be very useful for conducting an investigation. We have to try to reframe the case and actively look for new information. A new insight or some little known fact might change our entire frame of thinking. Professor Armstrong is right: The name of the game is the frame."

Phil always looked for some hidden pattern or an underlying motive when working on a particular case.

"Truth is more complex than the outward appearance," he would say. "Dig a little bit deeper and a different sense of reality will manifest itself. Most cops are looking at the specific events to solve a case. The actual mystery is in the complex relationships and the motivations of the players. Figure out the subtle interactions between the main characters and the case will solve itself!" Phil's fascination with human nature is what drove him to become a police detective. He was always curious, always looking for a new angle, always peeling another layer of perception, never tired of endlessly scrutinizing the same sequence of events.

"Phil, you should have been an accountant," I would tease him. "You never stop counting the beans—you analyze the same event or conversation repeatedly. Don't you get tired of it?"

Phil would chuckle. "I don't count the beans; I simply look at them. And these aren't ordinary beans—they're the jumping kind from Mexico! I just observe them as they dance back and forth—and lo and behold they change their shape! When I'm deconstructing relationships or identifying motivations in a case, a minor shift in my perception or an obscure new fact can cause a significant change in interpretation—a change that can lead to an entirely different angle or a new revelation. A small deviation in the frame can significantly alter my thinking process. No! It's not boring because every time I do it, there's a subtle change—it's always the first time!"

I now realized Phil had a good point—we should go over the events and relationships to discover new insights. I started thinking about recent events, trying to figure out what I had missed.

"Let's try to remember how we interacted with Laura during the last week. Maybe her behavior can provide some insight," I said.

"I know you blame yourself for not preventing her death," Phil countered. "I constantly castigate myself for the car accident with Mary Ellen. Your recollection of past events might appear vivid and accurate, but that's just an illusion. Your mind perceives and stores information selectively. I bet you're adding your present knowledge of Laura's death and revising your perceptions about past events. You're probably reading more into these events now with the advantage of hindsight. Stop kicking yourself. Try to look at past events without emotional guilt."

"Easier said than done. Can you look back at the car accident without guilt?"

I knew Phil was alluding to the *hindsight bias*. When we recall past incidents, present knowledge and our self-serving nature tend to contaminate our recollections. Normally, we tend to take credit for our past successes and rationalize our mistakes. But my guilt was compelling me to look for mistakes.

"I actually made a mistake," Phil said. "I don't think you made an error."

"We have to judge our own mistakes, don't we? It's difficult to assess our own frailties objectively. Avoiding guilt altogether is impossible."

There's no foolproof way to avoid the hindsight bias. When we try to recall any event, the first step is to recognize that the bias is always there. One way to improve the accuracy of our recollections is to keep a journal that records our impressions and perceptions at that time.

"Did you notice anything strange about Laura's behavior recently?" Phil asked.

"Laura had been stressed out in the last few weeks. I noticed that her hand would sometimes tremble. She was also concerned about Paul Gerber pestering her to go out with him. There was another weird thing Laura told me about Paul."

"What was it?"

"Laura mentioned that Paul Gerber was boasting about a secret chemistry club meeting. Something about an underground network. I don't remember anything more except that Clara was there, too, when Paul was talking about it. We should talk to Clara."

"Let's go back to the library right now; we can follow up with Clara," Phil accelerated his car.

* * *

When we went back to the library, it was as if time had stood still. The student was still sleeping in the reading room, only his snores had gotten louder. In the computer lab, the discussion had moved on to other topics. We did not want to interrupt the flow of the conversation, so we waited a few minutes and listened to the group. Clara, Raj, and John were listening to Stewart Anderson explain the viewpoint of his frame team.

"When we started to examine the role of patients and doctors," Stewart said, "we hit an immediate road block. What patients and doctors are supposed to do is not necessarily what all of them actually end up doing. In other words, their behavior is not always optimal. From my background in cognitive psychology, I know that patients are beset by conflict, doubts, and worry. They find relief by procrastinating, rationalizing, or shifting responsibility for their choices. Doctors may exhibit some of these traits, too."

Clara intervened, "Like what?"

Stewart replied, "One concept that comes to mind is *cognitive dissonance.*"

"Please don't give me some vague concepts," Clara rolled her eyes. "What, specifically, do you mean."

"New information and contradictions in our understanding generate cognitive dissonance or mental conflict. For instance, a patient might have a few episodes of dizziness. Although at some level, he may realize that something has to be done, he may allow this conflict—or dissonance—to build up without taking much action."

"We have some discomfort, but we still don't act?" Clara asked. "How could that be?"

"We try to reduce cognitive dissonance by rationalizing," Stewart said. "Sometimes we try to defer decisions by *defensive avoidance*—that's denying the new reality or indulging in some form of procrastination. The patient might rationalize that the episodes of dizziness aren't really that bad, or that he will see the doctor next month when he isn't so busy. Sometimes, we're held back by our prior beliefs and the comfort of a familiar existing situation. We're compelled to act only when our cognitive dissonance rises to an unacceptable level."

Raj chimed in: "Cognitive dissonance and defensive avoidance are quite prevalent. I read the case of an office supply company, Smart Office, which manufactures copy machines, among other things. In an initial consumer focus group, the executives detected a systematic flaw in the copy machine's design that resulted in paper jams. They were disturbed by these consumer reports, but they adopted several defensive avoidance strategies: the consumers did not follow directions adequately; the quality of the paper biased the test; let's wait for more feedback in the next production cycle. Their failure to confront the facts and change the design eventually had a high cost—the bad reputation of their defective product plagued Smart Office for years to come."

"How do these ideas relate to the Cicor case?" Clara asked.

Stewart consulted the notes in his laptop. "I can think of several ways cognitive dissonance and defensive avoidance may work. Normally, complications due to Cicor take time to manifest.

For instance, a disorder called rhabdomyolysis, which results in muscle breakdown, may take days or even weeks to be fatal. My research shows that some patients indulged in defensive avoidance and tried to deny the reality of their serious side effects. The cognitive dissonance was not strong enough to compel them to consult their doctor immediately. I hate to lay some responsibility on patients, but procrastination in this case can have fatal consequences."

"What about the role of doctors?" Raj asked. "They should ensure that patients understand all the potential complications."

"No doubt it's incumbent on doctors and pharmacists to explain all the side effects. Doctors were warned several times by PACE about possible complications. Specific warnings were issued about the significant increase in risk if Cicor is prescribed jointly with another medicine, Gemfibrozil. It appears that fifteen patients died because of the interaction between Cicor and Gemfibrozil. Doctors have to be more vigilant about all the potential interactions and side effects," Stewart said.

Raj added a different perspective: "I can't quarrel with the fact that doctors and pharmacists should closely monitor potential side effects. But doctors have to cope with a tremendous amount of paperwork in filing medical claims and dealing with HMOs. They are terrified of trivial lawsuits. Most of the new information comes in piece-meal fashion. The PDR is not updated adequately."

"PDR?" Clara raised her eyebrows.

"Their reference bible, the *Physician's Desk Reference*. Some critical information is bound to fall through the cracks. Doctors are trying to satisfice in a difficult situation."

"Did you say satisfy or satisfice?" Clara inquired.

Raj was apologetic. "I should have explained—the word is *satisfice*. We satisfice when we accept a result that is not optimal, but somewhat tolerable. We are overwhelmed with many changes and the relentless barrage of new information. We settle for a 'good enough' situation that we learn to accept. It is not surprising that some patients and doctors succumb to satisficing behavior. They find it difficult to look for optimal solutions when they are pressed for time. Indeed, given the cost of collecting and analyzing information, satisficing may be optimal in some cases."

Clara made a mock bow. "I have increased my vocabulary today with a new word: satisficing. I have to admit that satisficing behavior seems to be quite prevalent, don't you think?"

Raj nodded. "All of us indulge in some type of satisficing behavior to cope with the relentless changes in our environment. The executives of Smart Office were satisficing when they tolerated the defective design of the copy machine instead of insisting on better product quality. What compounds the problem for patients and doctors is that they don't have all the new information in a conveniently accessible form. I think we need a better Web site that consolidates and updates information about the potential side effects of new medicines. Doctors, pharmacists, and patients could all tap into the same Web site. Incentives for updating information should be provided. Otherwise many people may not make the effort to add new information to this Web site."

It was now close to lunchtime. As the students started drifting off, I took Clara aside. "Clara, I was wondering if you knew anything about the chemistry club Paul Gerber was talking about a few weeks ago."

Clara was surprised by the question. "I hardly know anything about it at all—I think Paul called it the 'Cocktail Hour.' I believe they have a local chapter, although I'm not sure if they're listed."

"Thanks, Clara. We'll see you later," I said.

As we came out of the library I said to Phil, "I'll try to find out more about the Cocktail Hour. I don't understand why the police aren't investigating Laura's case more aggressively. Is there a specific reason?"

"Shawn Douglas doesn't want to take any undue risks," Phil explained. "It's an understatement to say that the Armstrong family is influential in Chicago. Since Laura's room didn't indicate any foul play, Shawn used his discretion to rule the death as a suicide. He says he doesn't want to put the family through unnecessary anguish. Maybe the family has exerted some pressure. I don't know."

"What we've found out casts a different light on the case, don't you think?"

"Let's go someplace quiet and try to figure it out," Phil responded. "How about your room?"

* * *

When we walked into my campus apartment I had an idea. "Do you recall from our class readings how one of our founding fathers, Benjamin Franklin, used to make tough choices?"

"Something about making a balance sheet on a particular issue." Phil didn't seem thrilled.

"Ben Franklin used to write down the pros and cons of a difficult choice as he thought about an issue. It forced him to put all the pertinent information on either the pro or con side. He would ponder over the dilemma and discuss it with others, then add to his balance sheet. Once the list was complete, he would try to simplify it—cross out a pro and a con if they were almost of equal importance; balance two pros with one con if they were equivalent and cross them out. Eventually, his balance sheet would indicate whether the pro or the con side had more weight."

"If I remember correctly, Franklin explained his method to a friend in a letter. We're not sure how frequently he actually used the method. What's your point?"

"We can apply this process with a slight twist. Identify the pros and cons and assign weights to each, say from one—not important—to ten—very significant. We can add up the weights for all the pros and cons and see which side is more persuasive. At the very least, it will encourage us to be comprehensive and reflect on the advantages and disadvantages of our decision."

"Are you saying we should try this now?"

"Why not? What do we have to lose? We want to make sense of what we know about Laura's death, don't we?" I took a note pad from my desk and drew a line down the middle of the page. I wrote "Suicide?" at the head of one column and "Murder?" on the other.

Phil looked at the note pad. "All right, I guess we can give it a try. What are the main arguments that it was suicide? One reason could be that Laura felt guilty about her sister's death. She probably blamed herself for it."

In the suicide column, I wrote, "guilty about sister."

"What weight should we give to this aspect?" I asked. "I think she blamed herself more than she was letting on. How about an eight out of ten?"

Phil responded, "This weight part is subjective and tricky. Well, I guess an eight seems okay."

"She made travel plans on Saturday. That would go against the suicide argument. How about a weight of six for the travel plans in the murder column?"

Phil shook his head. "Six seems a bit low, let's settle on seven. No apparent sign of a struggle has to be a big one in the suicide column. The weight there should be a nine."

"I'll defer to your knowledge about the crime scene. How about possible suspects as an argument for murder? I can readily think of two persons. Donald Armstrong would make a fortune if his sister died first. Paul Gerber had some resentment against her, although I'm not sure exactly how much."

"The fact that some suspects are readily identifiable should be a pro for murder," Phil agreed. "The weight on this component should be high. A nine, I think."

As we bantered back and forth, our balance sheet took shape. The final tally came up like this:

BALANCE SHEET METHOD

Suicide?	Weights	Murder?	Weights
Guilty about sister	8	Made travel plans	7
No sign of struggle	9	Long phone call to Joan	8
Didn't take her pills	4	Possible suspects	9
Total	21	Total	24

Phil scratched his chin as he looked at the balance sheet. "This exercise has clarified our thinking, no doubt. But the weights are highly subjective. If we change the weights slightly, the suicide column might get heavier."

"You're right. The weights are difficult to judge." I thought about the casual way we had assigned them. "In some instances, we can justify the weights by obtaining objective data. But since our knowledge is incomplete, we're ascribing weights based on intuition. Subjective weights can be quite volatile. At least our discussion has developed some consensus about the importance of each factor. We were forced to think about all possibilities—to avoid knee-jerk reactions. This process works reasonably well for a decision involving two choices."

"Where does this leave us?" asked Phil. "I think we need to get more information to be sure. As Professor Armstrong often points out: Knowing what you don't know is progress."

"Do you think we have enough to persuade Shawn Douglas to conduct some kind of a medical exam? I realize an autopsy might be the last thing the Armstrong family wants. It's already Tuesday evening. You know there's a wake for Laura tomorrow night."

Phil was on his feet. "We have to act quickly. I'll tell Shawn about Laura's travel plans and her long phone call to Joan. It might persuade him to give me some latitude. Let's dig up more information about the circumstances of Laura's death."

9
Values and Facts

Everyone is a prisoner of his own experiences.
No one can eliminate prejudices—just recognize them.
—Edward Roscoe Murrow

A fter Phil left my room, I couldn't get Laura out of my mind. I glanced at the laptop that I had borrowed from her. Maybe something in the computer would provide a clue to her death. When I booted up the machine, I clicked on her e-mail. Laura was not a big fan of e-mail. There were about twenty-five messages that were still on the hard disk. No message had been archived. Most of the messages were replies to Professor Armstrong or Joan. Nothing noteworthy. One message had been sent to Donald Armstrong six days ago. I clicked on that message:

TO Armstrod@globaloptions.com

FROM Armstrol@andrews.edu

I didn't like our last discussion at all. I'm sorry I lost my temper. I find your attitude to be very condescending. You talk as if you definitely know what is best for me. Most of the time, I don't know what is good for me. How could you? Why are you trying to meddle in my affairs without appreciating what I am going through? Why do you have a negative opinion about Larry Rowe?
Let's meet soon to talk things over. Don't try to run my life—you are only driving a wedge between us. I wish you would allow me to make my own decisions. I can live with my own mistakes. Let's try to give each other some space, shall we? I love you.

I read the message twice—the second time more slowly. Apparently, there was some tension between Laura and her brother, Donald, and part of the argument seemed to be about me. I remembered how Donald had reacted when Laura introduced me at the Armstrong Awards night. His rude attitude made sense in the context of this e-mail. Maybe I was reading too much into it. Laura had not mentioned anything after the awards night. She was defending me on her own. This was vintage Laura—protecting others quietly and consistently.

I recalled an appointment I had made to see Professor Armstrong before the tragedy. Might as well keep it. I decided to walk to his office.

* * *

I strolled along the Plato toward Professor Armstrong's office building. It was an unusually warm day for the season. Spots of snow were melting in the sunshine, and beneath the patchy snow a green layer of moist grass was awaiting its turn. Spring had a way of defeating the winter gloom. It came in fits and starts until winter could not hold on to the cold winds. One could see it on the faces of the students who strolled around the campus: the anticipation that winter was about to give up was reflected in their warm smiles. But I could not shake off the winter chill lodged in my bones. Summer would be very different without Laura.

I tried to focus my mind on Professor Armstrong and the kind of questions he would ask in the discussion. What I admired about Professor Armstrong was his compassionate sense of justice. He provoked me to think about issues in a variety of ways. He challenged me to reexamine my moral perceptions about the way things are supposed to be.

"Put yourself in the other person's shoes," he would say. "Try to identify the reasons why a person acts in a specific way. You need to appreciate his constraints and his limitations. Don't be quick to judge. It's easy to judge, it's hard to understand, and it's difficult to change!"

I considered myself fortunate to have found Professor Armstrong as my mentor and intellectual guide. He was willing to offer his valuable time and energy whenever I needed it. Who needs a father when you can have a great professor guiding you every step of the way? I knocked on Professor Armstrong's office door. He was working on his computer. I glanced at the screen. A headline read "POLICY DILEMMAS FOR THE ASIAN CONTINENT."

"Professor Armstrong, do you still want to keep the appointment? We could do it some other day if you like."

Professor Armstrong turned toward me. His eyes had deep shadows. "No, Larry, let's talk today. It will keep us occupied. I know you were very close to Laura. It must be hard for you. There's so much suffering out there. How much can we control? How much suffering can we reduce?"

"I don't know about reducing the suffering of others. Right now, I'm in pretty bad shape myself. How are you coping with Laura's death?"

Professor Armstrong took a deep breath. He seemed to grow stronger as he inhaled deeply. "I try to focus on reducing the suffering of others who are in need of help. It reduces my own private pain about Laura's death. I find that helping others gives me a rationale to be alive—a rationale to do all the other crazy things I have to do to help them. What else is there?"

I ignored his rhetorical question. "By the way, thanks for the references on rationality. I tried to get a handle on the questions you raised. I assume that you're asking me why there isn't enough consensus on controversial issues, although we have some knowledge about them."

"Correct! I'm not referring to our ignorance, although it's monumental. I want to focus on the process of arriving at a consensus." Professor Armstrong looked at his screen as he talked.

"Both our subjective values and our perception of the objective facts enter into the arguments—right? Somehow both values and facts intertwine to create a Gordian knot. In fact, our subjective values color our view of the facts, don't they?" I was trying to pin down the basic problem.

"That's a good start, Larry. Take a controversial problem such as abortion and the stance taken by pro-life and pro-choice advocates. How would you decompose it?" Professor Armstrong turned around and faced me.

"Well," I answered, "proponents of the pro-life view start with a different set of values that focus on the child. The pro-choice arguments center on the mother. Both sides contend that they're trying to find the best solution for both the child and the mother, but their emphasis is somewhat different. One could build a strong belief system on either set of values."

"True. Let's not get into who's right or wrong. Both viewpoints could have a strong moral tone. Now, what about the facts?" asked the professor.

"The problem is that both sides view the facts from the perspective of their core values. Their value systems tend to influence their perception of the objective facts. Both sides have a different view of when life actually begins." I realized where he was going.

"Did you say objective facts? Is it possible to assess facts objectively?" Professor Armstrong raised his voice. I didn't want to get into the controversy of how we perceive reality. I ignored the bait.

"We have a better shot at assessing facts if we rely on the views of experts. I realize that they have a difficult time with it, too. But at least they're knowledgeable and they may be more objective."

Professor Armstrong stood up. "You may be right. If the experts can try to approach the issue in a bias-free manner and utilize the latest information, they have the best shot at marshalling facts. So where does this leave us? How do you build a consensus?"

The answer was dangling in the air. I grabbed it. "Try to separate the objective facts from the value systems. Let the experts sort out the objective facts in a bias-free manner to the extent that they can."

"And then what?" Professor Armstrong paced impatiently.

"Once the experts have ascertained the facts, they should present the objective information to the two groups of people who have different value systems. Their moral beliefs will still influence their perceptions about the facts, but both groups may realize that many of their differences are stemming from their core values rather than from the facts. Besides, there's a sizable silent majority in the center who are deeply disturbed by the extreme views of both the pro-life and pro-choice camps. A thoughtful moderate might argue that it's difficult to paint with a broad brush: Each case has its own complex set of choices."

Professor Armstrong stopped pacing, "You're right. Abortion is a difficult subject on which to build a consensus. The value systems are entrenched, and we're not very sure about the facts. But consider how a strong consensus on many divisive corporate issues can be attained by this method. Many business executives approach a complex issue with an entirely different set of values—values that are shaped by a variety of professional and cultural antecedents. If experts can help them arrive at a consensus about the facts, they may be able to trace most of their disagreements to differences in their values. We are not saying that looking at facts and values separately is a magic bullet, but we can decompose a complicated controversy in a meaningful way. You realize that although values and facts should be disentangled to gain better insight, in reality it's almost impossible to do so completely."

I nodded. "We can at least try to separate values from facts. I understand that it's just a way of trying to gain more insight."

Professor Armstrong returned to his computer screen. "All right. In the meanwhile, keep your spirits up. We all live with an internal beast that we have to learn to control somehow. Helping others is one way to tame this demon. If we look beyond our own needs, we can do so much to reduce suffering in the world. I need some good volunteers for an AIDS camp in Africa during the summer. Besides living costs, there's a modest stipend. Would you like to go?"

"I'm still trying to cope with Laura's death. I'll think about it and get back to you."

Professor Armstrong was already punching his keyboard when I slipped out of his office.

* * *

Phil called around 7:00 in the evening. "Larry, I explained to Shawn Douglas what we know. He agreed to let me arrange an informal medical exam on Laura."

"What does an informal medical exam entail?"

"I have to find a doctor who will go to the funeral parlor and examine Laura. Nothing is official. The doctor will look for any external evidence on the body. If we find something, Shawn may decide to follow up officially. At the present time, the official position is the same—Laura committed suicide."

"Phil, will you be able to get the medical exam done tonight?"

"I'm not sure—either tonight or first thing in the morning. But either way, please don't talk to anyone about what we're doing."

"Sure. But why?"

"I checked with Shawn to make sure it's okay that we're snooping around together. He said that as long as we keep it informal and strictly to ourselves, it shouldn't be a problem. I'll call you as soon as I get the exam done, okay?"

Phil didn't wait for a reply. The phone disconnected at the other end.

* * *

On Wednesday morning, it was show time. Some regular employees of GO had come to watch, and the GO conference room was crowded. Phil had not come to class. Donald and PACE executives sat in the middle with the three frame teams facing them. Professor Armstrong paced the periphery of the room.

"The frame teams have been researching the Cicor case for a while," Professor Armstrong began. "I understand the teams have been talking to each other and seeking clarifications from many sources. E-mails have been flying back and forth. Now it's time to consolidate. How do we solve this billion dollar corporate mystery? Remember, we have to formulate our recommendations for PACE. We have to ensure that they never again have to withdraw a promising new medicine like Cicor. Who'd like to fire the first shot?"

Clara had raised her hand before the professor had stopped talking.

"Our frame team came up with one recommendation. We understand that PACE has to ultimately recover all the money it's spending on research by marketing new competitive drugs. We also realize that PACE wanted to demonstrate that Cicor was more effective than other statins already on the market. However, PACE needs to reconsider its strategy of trying to obtain fast-track approval of higher dosages for new drugs. More is not always better. They need to carry out extended trials about the long-term benefits and risks of these drugs before pushing for higher dosages. PACE needs to evaluate short-term benefits along with the long-term risks."

Donald's tone was defensive. "Are you saying that PACE should just sit back and wait for these long-term studies to be completed? In the meanwhile, their competitors can reap high profits with the existing statins. Why don't you ask the other manufacturers to assess the long-term risk-benefit ratio? Why does PACE have to bear the burden alone?"

Professor Armstrong interjected, "A firm that introduces a new medicine has some obligation to take a long-term view. However, although individual firms may like to move on a fast track, the whole industry will benefit with a long-term perspective. Pharmaceutical industry leaders should devise better incentives to encourage their companies to cooperatively develop long-term assessment programs for new medicines. What can the FDA do in this regard?"

Raj spoke up, "The FDA could issue a more stringent warning about the side effects."

"But the FDA did issue warnings and sent out letters to the doctors," Professor Armstrong said. "Why were the warnings ignored?"

John Scott raised his hand. "I think psychology has something to do with it. Doctors get too many routine warnings—they tend to take these warnings in stride. They sometimes can't distinguish between routine warnings that are issued for liability purposes and more severe warnings that are dangerous to ignore."

"Good point, John. This demonstrates the importance of *signaling*. Doctors would benefit from a clear signal about the intensity of the danger rather than receive a plethora of vague ominous warnings. Every time concerns are raised about liability, a red-alert warning is printed. Doctors routinely ignore vague, shrill warnings because there are too many of them. Perhaps the FDA can classify the warnings by the intensity of the potential danger—a three-star warning would signal that ignoring the advice could be fatal. The FDA needs to ensure that the danger signals to the doctors about potential complications are limited and unambiguous. What other points?"

Raj responded, "Our frame team found that there is the possibility of a *sample bias*. The samples of patients employed in the FDA medical trials were not representative of patients at large. In reality, unlike the sample, most of the older patients are less healthy. On average they are taking two other prescription drugs. The sample of patients employed in the experimental trials should be more representative, otherwise PACE may not be accurately assessing risks in the FDA trials."

Professor Armstrong shot a glance at Raj and Donald. "Now we have a different suspect in this corporate mystery. Very sick patients may not have the luxury of waiting for long-term trials. For them, the potential benefits of the experimental drugs may outweigh unknown risks. Only a doctor can make this decision for a particular patient. Should we have a different set of trials for sicker patients compared to normal patients?"

Donald nodded. "I think PACE would consider that recommendation. There are two distinct issues. One is to ensure that for any medical trial the sample is an accurate representation of the patients at large. The other issue is to have separate studies for patients who are less healthy or have other complications. For them the incremental risk may be more severe."

"Good!" Professor Armstrong continued. "I guess we're going somewhere with this mystery. What else?"

Stewart volunteered. "We found many concepts in cognitive psychology that were helpful in discerning what went wrong. Some patients and doctors satisficed, others indulged in defensive avoidance to cope with the deluge of new information. The lack of *in-time information* about new side effects experienced by patients in different locations is a critical handicap. Establishing a centralized database on the Web may be a good way of updating, on a continuous basis, all the new information about drug side effects."

"Aren't there existing sites that provide information about the side effects of new medicines?" Professor Armstrong asked.

"Yes, but there's no common Web site that is neutral and frequently updated about emerging side effects," Stewart pointed out. "Besides, the databases of different pharmacy chains are not integrated to cross check for inconsistencies in prescriptions.

Patients searching for bargains often fill prescriptions at more than one pharmacy. A patient filling his prescriptions from different pharmacies may not be warned about the interaction between the drugs. We are always learning about new interactions with existing drugs. Incentives should be provided to patients, pharmacists, and doctors to integrate and update the data about side effects and safety on a centralized basis. What kind of incentives will work?"

Professor Armstrong walked toward the center of the room. "Incentives are needed, but if we offer large rewards for providing data, some people may fabricate information to obtain incentives. High incentives can often lead to perverse, unintended results. At one time in Europe, in order to curb bubonic plague, substantial rewards were given to find and kill rats. Some enterprising individuals started breeding rats—to kill them and collect the bounty!"

"What should be done?" Clara asked.

"Doctors keep records," said Professor Armstrong. "Doctors could be offered some modest incentives to maintain these records electronically. Part of the incentive for doctors is the ability to access an updated system of patient records from different offices. Concerns about patient privacy have to be addressed. Corporations and other interested parties could have access to the aggregate summary information without knowing the identity of patients. The important thing is to build an accurate database with the active participation from all the major players. Anything else?"

"How do we put all these issues together?" Stewart asked.

Professor Armstrong spread his hand out. "One thing is becoming clear about the Cicor case: This is not a simple mystery with one suspect. Reality is multi-faceted. There are plenty of suspects if we follow the trail. Consider this: If PACE executives frame the problem from *only their point of view,* they would inevitably draw narrow boundaries. Why is it important for PACE to adopt a *wide frame*?"

Raj replied, "A chain is judged by its weakest link. There were major concerns when patients died while taking Cicor, but no one waited to discover where the chain broke. Who was responsible for the failure? Everyone was rightly concerned about the likelihood of more deaths. Meanwhile, PACE was getting all the bad press. The company had to pull Cicor from the market and absorb a loss of more than a billion dollars. PACE has no choice but to frame the issue in a broad context."

Professor Armstrong ran his fingers through his beard. "Isn't that interesting? How a business problem can have many different dimensions? The behavioral responses of patients, pharmacists, and doctors are relevant. The regulatory framework of the FDA is relevant. Information constraints and incentives of the major players are relevant. If PACE considers only its *own* responsibility, it inevitably draws narrow boundaries and may court disaster. It is incumbent upon PACE to take into account the behavior of all other major players. The roles of doctors, pharmacists, patients, and the FDA have to be part of the framework. This is exactly what framing is about. This single insight will change the entire stack of options for PACE. The company will have to grapple with these concerns on a broad front. A new perspective, a wider frame has been generated."

Professor Armstrong was already walking out of the conference room as we scrambled to collect our books. I felt dejected and frustrated. We were not making adequate progress in Laura's case—but a new development was about to jolt our investigation.

10
Shortcuts that Undercut

It is interesting that humans try to find
meaningful patterns in things that are essentially random.
—Mr. Data, Star Trek, 1992

During the break on Wednesday morning, I kept thinking about Laura's death. Did Laura commit suicide? Was she murdered? I hoped Phil would get a clear answer today. My mind was in turmoil, waiting to hear, but Phil had not answered my phone calls.

After the break, John Scott made his presentation in class. He began in a hushed voice. "The way we assess chance events is subject to a variety of biases, some of them less obvious than others. Cognitive psychologists have obtained new insights into how we process information about uncertain events. Most of these biases are wired into our thinking as shortcuts. Evolution built these shortcuts in our minds to reduce information overload. These biases are pervasive, generally helpful, but often misleading. They can distort our thinking process."

Everyone was straining to hear John's whisper. Suddenly his voice grew in volume and intensity. "You may be familiar with the *gambler's fallacy*—a perception that sequential events are connected when they're actually independent of each other. Let's take a simple example. If a roulette wheel has not hit black for a long time, the perception grows that the wheel will 'correct itself' and the chances of hitting black will become higher. Assuming the wheel has not been programmed to hit particular spots, it has no memory. The results of the wheel are random. The chances of hitting black on any given spin of the wheel are always the same. *But we like to see patterns, because patterns make our lives understandable, so we tend to underestimate the role of chance."*

"I am not sure I get what you are saying," Clara raised an objection. "Sometimes systematic patterns do exist, don't they?"

John nodded. "Yes, Clara, they do. But we have to give random events their due. *Random streaks* are defined as systematic patterns in chance phenomena. These types of coincidences can occur quite frequently. If you flip a coin twenty times, for instance, there's about an 80 percent chance that you'll get three heads or tails in a row. That doesn't mean, however, that the same streak is going to be repeated. We have to realize that patterns we discern in past events are not *always meaningful."*

I was reminded of a financial example. Investors normally hunt for mutual funds that have the highest annual returns. However, most funds perform well for only two or three years, then other funds take over. It's likely that the managers of these high performing mutual funds are experiencing a lucky run. *The Wall Street Journal* conducts a competition between a portfolio recommended by financial experts and an alternative portfolio randomly constructed by throwing darts on a board. Quite frequently, the random portfolio generates a higher rate of return than the portfolio designed by experts. Perhaps there is no systematic pattern for predicting accurately the few mutual funds that will be lucky the next time. Looking for order in our lives is part of our instinct. But we should not read more into patterns than is warranted.

Phil sneaked into the classroom and sat behind me. He seemed agitated. I slipped him a note: *Did you learn anything new?*

Roller Coaster John's voice had reached a high pitch. "Sarah Liechtenstein, a psychologist who studies decision making, asked which kind of death is more common in the United States: murder or suicide? About 70 percent of the people replied that murder was more common. In reality, at that time, there were three suicides for every two murders. People regard murders as more frequent because they're reported prominently in the news media. This is an *availability bias:* We tend to think that something is more likely to happen if we can recall more instances of a similar event."

The public might think that murders are more common because of the availability bias, but what about the police? They are probably aware that suicides are relatively more frequent. It makes sense for someone to try to fool the police by faking a suicide.

Phil scribbled back: *The medical exam revealed that she has petechiae in her eyes.*

I tried to make sense out of Phil's note as John continued, "It's not surprising that your *own* experience influences probability estimates. You're likely to think that the chances of having a bankruptcy are higher if you've noticed more corporate failures in your own industry. People who have lived through the Great Depression of the 1930s tend to be more concerned about economic downturns. We have to guard against relying only on our limited ability to recall. Instead, we need to look at objective data."

"What kind of objective data are we talking about?" Clara asked.

John turned toward Clara. "We can try to estimate the underlying base rate. To get a reliable projection of the bankruptcy rate in the industry, we can count the number of bankruptcies declared by corporations compared to the overall number of firms in the sector. For business cycles, history tells us that a downturn has occurred at least once every eight to ten years. Good economic times haven't lasted forever. We need to ground our thinking in a broad historical context and look at actual data. That's why data series that extend far back in time are extremely valuable. We should avoid knee-jerk impressions that our mental shortcuts normally conjure up."

I scribbled another note to Phil: *What's petechiae in the eyes?*

John lowered his voice to a whisper. "Richard Thaler, an economist, described an imaginary person as shy, withdrawn, helpful, with a passion for detail. He then asked whether this person was a salesperson or a librarian? About two-thirds of the business executives guessed that the person was a librarian. Given the description, that may seem reasonable. But consider the fact that there are approximately eighty times more salespeople than librarians. Ignoring the statistics and focusing on the description of the individual leads us in the wrong direction. We tend to ignore the overall odds or base rates, and rely more on our immediate perceptions."

Stewart had another example: "We may fear traveling by plane because we don't have any direct control. Many atrocious terrorist incidents have heightened our fears about air travel. On the other hand, we feel very comfortable behind the wheel of our trusty car. However, in terms of accidents and fatality rates per mile, traveling by car is many times more dangerous than flying. Most of us don't evaluate risk objectively."

Raj raised his hand. "Let us consider how these insights apply to PACE's problem with Cicor. Out of the eighty patients who died while taking Cicor, some could have died due to other factors or chance events—we have to discern whether the pattern of their deaths had any other plausible explanation. Many of these patients would have died anyway because of other complications regardless of whether they took Cicor."

"Have you calculated the base rates?" Scott asked.

"Yes, the base rates are quite different than the prevailing perceptions. The fact that many of these deaths were publicized by the media resulted in an availability bias—a perception that many more deaths were likely," Raj replied. "Consider the reality that more than one million patients were taking Cicor. From my research, it seems approximately fifty deaths can be attributed directly to the medicine. That is fifty out of a million patients or a probability of 0.00005. That is a fairly low chance, don't you think?"

"That chance might appear low to you from a statistical point of view," Clara said indignantly. "I bet you would have a different opinion if you or one of your family members were one of these fifty patients. The unnecessary death of even one patient is a tragedy for the family and for society at large."

Phil's reply came back: *Petechiae are tiny hemorrhages in the whites of the eyes—she was probably suffocated!*

A tight sensation gripped my chest. I tore Phil's note and crumpled the pieces into a ball. My fingers compressed the ball into a tight wad. I could not focus on the class discussion. A disturbing picture kept intruding: Laura's eyes widening as someone choked her—she was trying to cry out for help but no sound escaped from her mouth.

Raj raised his hand. "I understand these shortcuts are coping mechanisms—a way to reduce stress when faced with information overload. Other biases such as defensive avoidance and satisficing also try to relieve pressure. We know that these types of biases and shortcuts lead to suboptimal decisions. Can we reduce stress in more useful ways?"

Professor Armstrong shrugged his shoulders. "We have to recognize that decision making is inherently stressful. In our professional and personal lives, we live with cognitive dissonance, we practice defensive avoidance, and we often satisfice. We try to alleviate the psychological pressure of decision making by adopting shortcuts. One way to handle pressure is to harness the soothing powers of a systematic routine—always take a few calm methodical steps."

"How do you actually do it?" Clara asked.

Professor Armstrong shrugged his shoulders again. "I can't tell you exactly what to do. You know the biases that are common traps in your own mind. You can fine tune the method based on your own needs. Corporations can develop a systematic process for arriving at critical decisions—a process that acknowledges and addresses their limitations and that builds on their strengths. There can be a healthy competition within a business organization for new ideas and innovative strategies. For important decisions, when time is on your side, consider the following steps:

- Define your goal as precisely as you can; try to be specific.

- Make sure you are well informed; collect more information if you have doubts.

- Develop a range of alternatives; generate new ones if needed.

- Don't jump in; pick a course of action with careful deliberation.

- After the decision, look closely for feedback to reassess your strategy."

"What do you mean by careful deliberation?" Clara persisted.

"To deliberate carefully we should follow a systematic routine. The Balance Sheet method is convenient for evaluating a variety of decisions that involve two options. If we are trying to decide between two competing designs for a new product, we can sort out the pros and cons by this method. Evaluating the aggregate total for each option will indicate which design is more persuasive. The method can be employed to evaluate alternative marketing strategies. For decisions involving more than two alternatives, we'll talk about two other procedures: WARS and Scenario Strategies."

I couldn't listen to the class discussion any more. Laura's silent scream reverberated in my mind. The class was scheduled to end in twenty minutes anyhow. I mouthed to Phil, *Let's get out of here.* He nodded slightly. As we sneaked out, I tossed my crumpled paper ball in the trashcan. Professor Armstrong's voice boomed, "Don't forget the mantra—recite it again and again..." as I gently closed the back door of the classroom.

I tried to digest the news about Laura's medical exam. "Why didn't the medical examiner find out about petechiae in Laura's eyes on Monday morning when they found her?"

"The medical examiner didn't do a comprehensive exam on Monday because Shawn was rushing things. He kept saying that there didn't appear to be any foul play. He was not actively questioning his presumptions."

"Does this mean that we're now dealing with a murder for sure?"

"Shawn has changed his tune. He's demanded a full autopsy before Laura's wake. By this evening we should have the full report. Petechial hemorrhages in the whites of the eyes are usually caused by a lack of oxygen. In Laura's case, the ruptures were tiny. The lack of bruises on her body implies that somebody might have choked her suddenly—with precision and force. A soft object, probably a pillow, suffocated her."

My mind raced through different scenarios. Who could have walked into her campus apartment? Was there a strong motive? Maybe we were missing a big part of the puzzle. We had to do something.

"What can we do now?" I said.

"Shawn is the chief detective in charge of the investigation. Soon this is going to explode in the press. In the meantime, he's allowed us to snoop around a little. Shawn figures he owes me on this one."

"Where shall we go, Holmes?" I asked half in jest and half in exasperation.

Phil's pace quickened. "Let's talk to some people who were around Laura's room. A maid cleans in Laura's building; let's find her. The game is afoot!"

* * *

"Larry, you read too many Sherlock Holmes books when you were a kid, didn't you? How could someone kill Laura and leave no trace of the crime?" Chris can't contain his excitement.

"If it was indeed murder, either the murderer or an accomplice could have removed all incriminating evidence. We had to reframe the issue; try to picture different scenarios. But before I get into that part of the story, what do you think about the shortcuts John Scott was talking about?"

"These psychological biases are fascinating. I remember some instances when I tried to make a pattern out of something that didn't have one. In baseball, when I have struck out several times in a row, I tend to think my lucky streak will return after a while. If we're playing at the same level, each time at bat is a random event, isn't it? Have you learned how to avoid these biases?"

"The first step is to be aware of them. Realize that we can succumb to these biases, instinctively and inadvertently. I find myself falling into these mental traps all the time. I tend to think that something is more likely to happen just because I'm able to recall events similar to it. I try to stop myself in mid-stride and find out about the underlying odds."

"Are using anchors always bad?"

"No, as long as we recognize what anchors are doing to our thinking and try to be objective about other biases that may creep in. For instance, when my company evaluates alternative projects, the cost of borrowing the funds becomes an inevitable anchor. That's a reasonable threshold: to predict the net rate of return of a proposed project over and beyond the prevailing interest rate. But we found our thinking was influenced by a subtle bias. When we identified a project that met this criterion, we had a tendency to satisfice—to settle for a project simply because the return

*was 3 or 4 percent higher than the interest rate. Lately, we have raised
our expectations. We diligently conduct a broader search to find the few
projects that are more profitable without incurring additional risk."*

"What else can you do?"

*"We have to develop our own strategies to combat these biases. If we
fight the battle vigilantly, eventually our thinking will become more clear
and objective. The important thing is to keep improving and move along
the learning curve. All of us are fallible, but some of us end up on a higher
plain of knowledge and awareness."*

*Chris picks up a newspaper. "I remember reading about many
lawsuits against PACE. Something about new information surfacing in
court cases. You guys didn't have all the information when you were
analyzing the case, did you?"*

*"You are right, Chris, we did not have access to more recent corporate
information. Now it is clear that PACE executives were trying to increase
the market share of Cicor from 10 to 20 percent. They wanted Cicor to
achieve a blockbuster status—somehow a 20 percent market share had
become an anchor for them. Information about adverse reactions from the
medicine that was beginning to trickle into the corporate offices was not
fully investigated. The ultimate impact was one hundred deaths from
complications and more than ten thousand lawsuits."*

"That is a lot of lawsuits. How did they react to all this pressure?"

*"We know now that some of these lawsuits were frivolous—others
were quite legitimate. PACE adopted an effective two-pronged strategy.
They decided to settle about two thousand cases where they thought Cicor
probably caused serious harm. On the other hand, they aggressively
fought claims that were deemed as marginal or frivolous. They developed
a confidential table indicating the amount of compensation they were
willing to pay for each type of injury. PACE's strategy of divide and conquer has become a model for limiting overall product liability litigation."*

*Chris shifts to a different topic. "I'm confused about values and facts.
You say it's impossible to separate values from the facts, but we should
still try to do it to develop a better understanding of a problem. Are you
saying that values and facts are always intertwined?"*

*"Yes, Chris, it's almost impossible to separate our values from facts.
Every person has a core set of values. Our values act as a filter—any fact
that we perceive and evaluate is refracted through this filter. It's easy to
think that we can suspend judgment, but judgment is rarely suspended.*

It's important to be conscious of our values and how they influence our 'objective' evaluation. Understanding the interaction between values and facts can improve our insight and help us in building a consensus."

"Okay! Larry, enough of this stuff! Tell me if you guys talked to the maid."

"Yes, we did. Before we get to that, I have to tell you about the conversation I had with Phil. Our minds were kicking into high gear. New ways of looking at the problem were opening up...."

I want to relive every minute of that season of all seasons.

11
Dissect the Suspects

Caesar: *Let me have men about me that are fat;*
Sleek-headed men, and such as sleep o' nights:
Yond Cassius has a lean and hungry look;
He thinks too much: such men are dangerous.
—Shakespeare,
***Julius Caesar*, Act 1, Scene II**

A s we walked toward the campus apartments, Phil rambled.
"I think we can start with the assumption that Laura was murdered. We'll know for sure after the autopsy later today. But if we hadn't actively looked for contrary evidence, the presumption of suicide would have prevailed. Once the body was buried, it would be difficult to prove anything. Questioning our assumptions has changed our entire frame. It pays to be a contrarian."

I joined the thought process. "One way to develop a flexible frame is to assume that the final result has happened, and try to *generate multiple scenarios* that may lead to the final event. Once we assume that Laura was murdered, we can imagine many more scenarios of how the murder took place. What kind of scenarios would lead to her murder?"

Phil walked briskly. "One boundary we can draw around our frame is this: It was probably an inside job! There were no broken windows or doors, no sign of a struggle. Laura probably knew the person who came into her room. It's likely she was caught by surprise—that would explain the lack of any struggle."

"Then, given that it's someone she knew, we need to start from the basics of any police investigation—motive, means, and opportunity. First, think of motives. Who would benefit from Laura's death? Donald Armstrong gets all the family fortune. He's doing well, but greed has no limit. Besides, he's cold and manipulative," I said.

"I agree that Donald is a creep. Do you know what happened to the return on his portfolio recently?"

"No, I don't. How did you get information about his portfolio?"

Phil smiled. "Let's just say a friend at Merrill Lynch has been talkative lately. Anyway, Donald has a massive portfolio in aggressive growth stocks. The annual return on his portfolio was around 25 percent for three years. Last year was an exception. His portfolio actually went down by 15 percent. That might make him more greedy, don't you think?"

"It could, but I'm sure Donald is aware of the *regression to the mean*."

"Regression to the what?" Phil asked.

"Regression to the mean or the average, Phil. In the nineteenth century, a British scientist, Sir Francis Galton, found that very tall fathers generally had sons who were shorter. On the other hand, very short fathers had sons who were relatively taller. Succeeding generations were regressing toward the average height of the population. Applied to investments, after an unexpectedly good performance over several years, a portfolio's earnings rate will fall back toward the mean—simply because long runs of good luck are rare."

"I see your point. Donald shouldn't be expecting an annual return of 25 percent every year. Very good years have to be followed by some bad years. In Donald's case, in spite of last year's drop of 15 percent, the four-year mean works out to an annual return of 15 percent."

I switched topics. "What about Paul Gerber? Laura definitely irritated him. Does irritation constitute a strong enough motive?"

"He has an explosive temper," Phil agreed. "I can visualize Paul going to Laura's room on some pretext. Maybe he pulled an Armstrong—made a clumsy proposal and she refused. What if his pent-up resentment exploded suddenly? We can't rule that out. Remember what he did to that chair!"

"Paul Gerber clumsy with girls? I doubt that, Phil. He's too smooth. You're right about his anger being unpredictable, but I can't imagine him pulling an Armstrong."

"Pulling an Armstrong" had an interesting history. The story about Professor Armstrong's relationship, or I should say the lack of a relationship, with a girl called Amber had become a legend in the corridors of St. Andrews. Many different versions of the tale floated around. With all the retelling, it was hard to figure out what parts of the story had been exaggerated. A sanitized version of the story went something like this:

In his freshman year at Harvard University, Professor Armstrong was hopelessly smitten by Amber, a striking girl in his debating club. She had won a prestigious debating contest with Yale that year. Professor Armstrong did not know how to profess his love to her. For years, he nursed his affection and tried to be around her. He would go to the same clubs and classes that Amber had joined and hover around in the background. His feelings grew stronger yet his tongue could not articulate any words. All his youthful energy, his dreams, what he wanted to be were focused on Amber, but she was not even vaguely aware of it.

One cold winter morning, while Professor Armstrong was walking through Harvard Square with Amber and other students, he could not control his pent-up emotions any longer.

"Amber, I have something to tell you," he said.

"What is it, Martin?" Amber did not break her stride.

He dropped to his knees on the muddy grass and, stretching out his hands, exclaimed, "Come! Live with me and be my shepherd, and we will all pleasures prove!"

Amber did not blink an eyelid. "Oh! Martin! Get off the muddy grass. You are so nerdy but sooo cute!"

Then she walked off, talking to the captain of the basketball team. Professor Armstrong's world came tumbling down. He struggled to his feet and went back to his dormitory. He did not leave his room for two days. When he finally emerged, he talked to no one. For six whole weeks, he went about his classes without uttering a single word.

He became the butt of many campus jokes. When students wanted to caution somebody about a clumsy date proposal, they would say, "Don't pull an Armstrong!" And thus Professor Armstrong contributed to the evolving lexicon of Harvard campus life. But he did wipe his muddy knees in Harvard Square that day, and he did not forget. When in the company of women, he is always gracious and charming, but legend has it that he never again seriously considered a relationship with a woman.

The sharp cold wind made us walk faster. Phil took quick long strides as we cut across the campus to the student apartments. A thin layer of snow had fallen. Footprints in different directions revealed the shortcuts students had taken. The footprints left pockmarks on an otherwise pristine face.

"Are there any other suspects we can consider?" I asked.

"What about Professor Armstrong?" Phil's voice was low and even.

"What about him?" I stopped walking. The thought was crazy. Professor Armstrong couldn't be a suspect. What motive could he have? Phil waved his hand to signal we should keep walking.

"Remember the *halo effect*?" Phil cautioned. "The notion that we tend to see things in clusters. Policemen appear taller because they represent authority. A business executive driving an expensive car is also perceived to be well dressed. A professor has to be a man of virtue. We distort reality by ascribing the same properties to all things that are in the same cluster."

"We shouldn't rule him out just because he's a professor, I agree. But what motive would he have?"

"I don't know. He's an uncle to both Donald and Laura. Maybe he gets the money if they both die. Remember Professor Armstrong's own refrain: Don't draw narrow boundaries—the solution might elude you. We shouldn't exclude anyone at this point."

"I agree we should have a broad frame, but Laura indicated that Professor Armstrong gives most of his money to charity. Greed could hardly be a motive." I thought this conversation was going nowhere.

"Motive alone doesn't do the trick," Phil said. "We have to look at the time of death and scope out the alibis. I'll dig up the medical examiner's report about the time of death. That will be the place to start."

The maid was cleaning a room two doors from Laura's apart-ment. She was a tall, Hispanic woman, with many lines etched in her face—not the wrinkles that come from age, but the ones brought about by suffering and hard work. Her skin tone was vibrant and healthy. I didn't think she was past thirty-five years old. As we approached her, she seemed to deliberately ignore us. Phil took out his badge and explained that we had a few questions. When she saw the police badge her face lost some color.

"What do you want to know?" she asked hesitatingly. She twisted the edge of her apron, as she looked sideways at us.

"We know your name is Angela," Phil said gently, stepping back to give her some space. "You're in charge of cleaning Laura Armstrong's room. When was the last time you saw her?"

"I cleaned her room around noon on Saturday. She was not in her room. I saw her the day before, on Friday," Angela replied, gaining more confidence.

"Did you clean her room on Sunday?"

"No, Sunday is my day off. I did not come here on Sunday." She had tied the edge of her apron into a knot.

"Okay, Angela. Is there anything else you noticed that might be unusual?" Phil asked.

"No. I just do my work. Can I go back to work now?" She was already moving back to her task.

"All right. Thanks, Angela. Here's my card. Call me if you think of something." Phil handed his card to her as we left.

"Something is wrong here," Phil said as we walked back to my apartment. "I can't put my finger on it, but she seemed very uncomfortable."

"Many immigrants are leery of police officers. In the old coun-try, there's often an abuse of authority and no rule of law. It's not surprising that they develop a fear of government officials. On the other hand, maybe she's hiding something."

"Maybe. I'll try to check up on her."

Later in the evening, Phil and I sat on an oversized sofa in my room munching sandwiches. My normally untidy room had attained a new level of chaos. Dirty dishes from three days were stacked in the sink. Books overflowing from the table lay scattered on the floor. Unlike Laura, I had elected not to have a daily maid service. Now I could not bring myself to clean my apartment. Laura had moved some of the things out of place during her last few visits. I had to maintain the disorder. Part of Laura was still in the room. Phil called Police Headquarters to get the medical report about the time of Laura's death. I was trying to find some information about Paul Gerber.

My laptop blinked, "You have mail!" I clicked the receive mail icon, and a message popped out:

YOU GUYS ARE HOT TO TROT! PAUL GERBER IS A WOLF IN SHEEP'S CLOTHING. THE PAST PORTENDS THE FUTURE.

A FRIEND.
PEEPING TOM

Phil stared at the screen, trying to digest the message. "Can you find out who sent this?" His voice rose in excitement.

I looked at the message; the author of the mail was indicated as tompeep@fastserve.net.

"I guess Peeping Tom is a nickname. Maybe we can trace the computer from where the message was sent."

"Print out the message and give me the details of your server, Larry. I'll try to get it traced. Is this person trying to lead us to Paul Gerber as a suspect? How does he even know we're investigating? The word isn't out yet."

"Could be someone in the police force, or someone who over-heard our conversation. It's confusing no doubt—we have to keep our heads."

"Yes, Larry. Remember Kipling:
　　'If you can keep your head when all about you
　　Are losing theirs and blaming it on you,
　　If you can trust yourself when all men doubt you,
　　But make allowance for their doubting too.'
I like the part about making allowances for other people's doubts."

"Kipling puts too much weight on certainty," I said. "Trusting yourself completely is almost impossible—doubt isn't necessarily a bad thing. We have to make allowance for each other's doubt and discuss things. We can move toward more certainty as we get more facts."

"Stop picking apart an inspiring poem, will you?" Phil retorted. "Don't contaminate Kipling's inspired lines with your morbid analysis."

Phil was joking, but his voice betrayed tiredness and an anxiety that was uncharacteristic. He rose to leave.

"Anyway, let's find out about the alibis, Larry. Why don't you look up Donald Armstrong and I'll try to find out about Paul Gerber. Just make a few discreet phone calls. Don't confront anyone directly. I'll talk to you in the evening."

I didn't have time to react; Phil was already out the door. He was about to discover some surprising leads.

12
Track the Feedback

Life is like playing a violin in public
And learning the instrument as one goes on.
—Samuel Butler

O n Wednesday night, I didn't feel like reading. My thoughts kept going to Laura's lifeless body. I needed a diversion. Reluctantly, I picked up Professor Armstrong's notes.

> After choosing a tentative line of action or even while making a decision, you have to track and listen to your feedback. Before you make your choice, every decision is an opportunity. After the decision is made, we have another opportunity—an opportunity to learn. Since decision making is a process, you need to be vigilant: keep your ears to the ground at all times. You can get feedback even while making the decision—one doesn't preclude the other. Making decisions and actively listening to feedback should be regarded as an integrated process.
>
> If a decision is not going to be repeated, listen closely to all the fallout from your choice. Evaluate and update your learning with feedback. If the decision has to be repeated, try to establish a procedure to obtain feedback on a regular basis.
>
> Consider an example: strategy for introducing a new product. You can get feedback while making the decision. Conduct a pilot test with likely customers to develop the product before you introduce it in the market. When the product is sold, survey your customers periodically. Find out what aspects of the product consumers liked. What can you

change in the item to improve customer satisfaction? Give your customers an incentive to provide feedback. The secret of marketing is being close to your customer. The mantra: Track and listen to your feedback.

I took a swig of my Mountain Dew® to keep me awake. Professor Armstrong had a good point: Making the decision first and getting feedback later created a false dichotomy. Getting more information about the suspects was an example of ongoing feedback. We should continue to refine our judgments about the suspects as we went along. Continuously combining feedback and decision making made sense. We had to keep collecting more information about the suspects and fine tuning our decision process. I read on:

Here is one complication of feedback:

Part of your feedback may be left out. Even if you conduct a periodic survey, you may be neglecting a whole class of information. Consider an example. You're an admissions officer at an elite college. You can easily know how the students you admitted have performed. What about the performance of the students you didn't admit? Have you tried to get any feedback on those who were denied admission? What about the candidates you admitted but who decided to go elsewhere? This is *overlooked feedback*. Half the story may be missing!

Tracking some of those you didn't admit or who went to a different school could provide invaluable insight into your decision-making process. Maybe you have been overlooking something all along without noticing it. Comparing the profiles of the students you admitted with those who went elsewhere may indicate that one of your admissions criteria is unreliable. Perhaps you're not paying enough attention to the non-academic achievements of students.

Here is another example. You routinely track how the design of a new product has influenced your sales. How about obtaining feedback about the designs you didn't adopt? Can you develop a pilot test or a modest survey to discover the potential impact of the designs you didn't adopt? Looking at the shelved designs will give you a benchmark. You can use this benchmark to evaluate the impact of the designs you have adopted.

I rubbed my eyes. There was something useful here. We should be trying to figure out the gaps in our knowledge about the suspects. Once we identified overlooked feedback, we could obtain additional information. My thoughts drifted to Donald Armstrong. What did I really know about him? Laura hadn't revealed a whole lot about her brother. We could try to check out the background of the suspects on the Internet—many details find their way to the Web. But what about other information that is not picked up by the Web search engines? We could be overlooking feedback from a whole class of information. I made a mental note to check for any additional information about Donald from friends who worked at GO.

I moved to the next paragraph:

Another complicating factor about feedback is *treatment effects*. Take an example: You want to hire a salesperson. You are trying to analyze the true marketing potential of different sales personnel. In the past, some salespeople who exceeded their quotas were given hefty bonuses. This reward system encouraged them to work even harder and beat their new sales targets. Are these salespersons *inherently* better at their jobs than the others? Or did they perform better because they were "treated" differently? The answer is probably a combination of both factors. The subtle influence of treatment effects tend to distort the accurate measurement of each person's marketing potential.

Treatment effects are widespread. A teacher identifies high achievers and gives them more attention. Is their subsequent achievement due to their own effort or is it because of the *additional* attention by the teacher? It's hard to disentangle the two effects. Veiled treatment effects may distort feedback.

I walked to the kitchen sink and splashed cold water on my face. Once word got out that Laura was murdered, it would be difficult to obtain accurate feedback. The suspects would realize that they were being observed. This very realization would alter their behavior. The actual perpetrator might be able to disguise his or her guilt more effectively. Other suspects who are a focus of the inquiry will probably become defensive and angry. How police officers and others treat the suspects will cause subtle changes in their behavior. This whole notion of entwined feedback made everything more complicated.

My thoughts shifted to PACE—this information about feedback was important for the Cicor case. We are constantly learning about new complications of a drug throughout its life cycle. A recent study by Georgetown University researchers indicated that 21 percent of the drugs that had come to the market had their dosages reduced subsequently. Consequently, PACE had to collect relevant information from patients, doctors, and the FDA, as well as monitor the behavior of competitors on an ongoing basis. It wouldn't be a good strategy for PACE to view information gathering and decision making as two distinct phases. Collecting feedback and developing a viable strategy had to be a simultaneous process.

Instead of focusing its entire attention on drugs like Cicor that had problems, PACE should investigate why other comparable new drugs were successful. A comparative analysis may unearth some critical aspects in the successful drug programs that PACE had ignored in the Cicor case. Maybe the samples of patients employed in the successful programs were more representative of the population at large. Perhaps the successful programs monitored patients for a longer period. If executives at PACE focused only on the drugs that had problems, they could miss a whole class of relevant information.

The ringing of the phone interrupted my thoughts. It was Phil.

"Hey! Sorry I snapped at you. I could say I was too tired but that would be a poor excuse."

"It's all right, Phil, you don't have to apologize. What's the scoop? Anything new?"

"Aren't you going to Laura's wake tonight?"

"I can't go, Phil. I hate the formality of a wake. To look at her dressed up in a box is too much to bear. I don't feel like talking about her with acquaintances. I'll try to say my farewell in my own private way."

Phil sensed my anguish. He didn't press me further. "The least we can do for Laura is to try to nab her killer. I don't know how far we'll be able to go. Let's get back to business. What do you want first—the good news or the bad news?"

"Why don't you *split up the good news and combine the bad news*." I recognized the game Phil was playing. According to cognitive research, gains should be split up due to the diminishing satisfaction of each additional gain. It's always better to provide gains in small pieces, so as to increase the recipient's overall satisfaction. Advertisers on television offer many small things packaged individually, all available "If you order now!" Each small goodie packaged separately increases the customer's overall satisfaction. On the other hand, losses are painful and should be combined in one swoop—otherwise, it's like Chinese water torture.

"Let me give you the good news in stages," Phil warmed up to the game.

"I found a reason why Angela might be uncomfortable. She was in the dorms on Sunday. One of the students saw her around 7:00 that night. She seems to be hiding something."

"What else?"

"Here's a big one. I checked the police records in Paul Gerber's hometown, Providence, Rhode Island. Looks like Paul had a prior that was officially expunged from his record." Phil tried to drag it out.

"What was it?"

"Nothing in the official record. I called the precinct and snooped around. It was something about beating up a student in high school. Apparently, Paul's bullying got out of control and one person was badly hurt. The case eventually went to juvenile court. The person I talked to didn't want to get involved."

"At least we know that he's capable of violence." I tried to picture Paul Gerber beating up a smaller kid.

"Now on to Donald Armstrong, if he's the sole surviving heir, eventually he gets all the family fortune. But not until he's thirty-five. If he's not around, the whole estate goes into an administered trust. I guess his motive is pretty strong."

"Any other good news?" I was getting used to Phil's ability to dig up facts.

"Only the bad news. We traced the computer message that you received to your server bank on Prodigy. They checked where the message came from. It was sent from one of the computers in the Harold Washington Public Library. Apparently, you don't need to provide accurate identifying information to send a message on the Internet. So although we know the computer that the message was sent from, we won't know who sent it." Phil's voice sounded dejected.

"What about Peeping Tom's server? Doesn't the server have details about who signed up for the account?"

"Good point. The particular server doesn't verify the information when someone signs up for a free e-mail account. All the information used to sign up for the account was probably fictitious anyway."

"The sender did try to keep his identity a secret although his tip about Paul Gerber was useful. If he's a friend, why go through this roundabout way of sending a message?"

"We are not sure this person is a male, are we? The sender may not want to be questioned. Sending an anonymous message ensures that he or she won't get involved. Maybe the message is meant to throw us off track. There might be other motives, hard to say for sure." Phil stopped abruptly: "Hey, gotta go. Talk to you first thing in the morning."

I had to look up the background information for Donald, so I booted up Laura's laptop. In the search function space, I typed, "DONALD + ARMSTRONG".

I got 9,813 hits. Some of the Donald Armstrongs were in Atlanta and San Francisco. I refined my search: "DONALD + ARMSTRONG + GO + CORPORATION + NEWS + REPORTS".

This time there were 841 hits, some going back nine years. Almost all of them related to Donald or GO. That's the trouble with search engines—they give you everything you don't need. It was going to be a long night sorting through this haystack. I opened up another bottle of Mountain Dew, yawned one more time, and got to work. I knew there was some information out there I could not afford to miss.

13
Verify the Alibi

If we begin with certainties, we shall end in doubt;
but if we begin with doubts, and are patient, we shall end in certainties.
—Francis Bacon

O n Thursday morning, Phil handed me the medical examiner's report. I read the section about the time of death:

Estimated Time of Death

At the scene of death, these observations were made at 7:35 Monday morning. The corpse had cooled from the regular temperature of 98.6 F (37 Celsius). Normally, a body cools at one degree Celsius per hour for the first 12 hours. Room temperature was at 22 Celsius. Rectal temperature was 29.5 Celsius. These two base points indicate that death occurred within a 6–10 hour time window.

Liver mortis is in most cases completely developed and permanent within 8–12 hours. In the subject case, lividity was approximately 75% complete. This is consistent with the 6–10 hour window.

Onset and completion of rigor mortis can occur anywhere between 0–34 hours. Body indicated mild signs of an early stage of rigor mortis. Since it is difficult to assess if instantaneous rigor has been a factor, this variable was not given prominence in evaluation.

Based on these preliminary findings, the time of death is deemed to be between 10:00 p.m. Sunday and 2:00 a.m. Monday.

I winced at the cold writing style. The graphic description of the murder released my acid valves all over again. Phil looked over my shoulder as he spoke.

"You should read on. The doctor has a zinger about buying a software program to estimate the time of death. That's a cover-your-back strategy." I looked at where he was pointing:

Note: The time estimates are approximations given the room temperature and position of the body. I have frequently indicated that the Forensic Department needs to install a Death–Time Software Program.

This software program assesses time of death, relying on inputs from more than six criteria. The program evaluates the information inputs based on well-established benchmarks from forensic research. It is designed to detect warnings about input errors and contradictions. This program was used in the O.J. Simpson trial in 1995.

My budget request for the program, developed by the forensic institute in Essen, Germany, in collaboration with Professor Henssge, is pending with the Finance Department. Output from this program, combined with the intuitive judgment of the medical examiner, will generate a more comprehensive and reliable evaluation of the likely time of death.

Dr. Robin Murdoch
Medical Examiner

"Dr. Murdoch is right about the software, Phil. Research shows that decision models that rely on objective historical data are quite accurate. Based on benchmarks developed by previous experience, the computer model can evaluate different variables that go into the decision. This analysis systematically uses all pertinent objective information. As an expert, Dr. Murdoch can check the results of the computer model and bring his intuitive judgment into play. The final decision about the time of death based on a combination of objective data analysis and subjective judgment is probably the best process. In class, we dubbed it the M&M approach—*Man and Machine*."

"I understand the subjective judgment part, but what do you mean by the machine?" Phil asked.

"Most computer models use canned statistical packages such as SAS or STATA, to name a few. These menu-driven packages can analyze the data using a variety of different forecasting methods. Consider the case of business forecasting. We can generate a statistical forecast with these packages based on the latest business data. Alternatively, we can survey business executives and economists about their subjective expectations. The results of the statistical model formalize historical patterns that may repeat in the future. The survey results capture qualitative factors such as intuition and experience of the experts. Combining both approaches makes sense."

Phil nodded. "My doctor once assessed my risk for heart disease. He took my numbers for blood pressure, cholesterol, age, height, weight, incidence of heart disease in the family, and computed a risk score based on people who had profiles similar to mine. He told me my numerical score was 1.2, on a scale of 0 to 9, where 0 indicated no risk. After that, he asked me about my lifestyle and food habits. Eventually, he scratched his head and gave me a clinical assessment that my risk for heart disease was very low. I suppose he was doing the same thing you're talking about—combining objective analysis with subjective judgment."

My mind drifted back to the technical information in the medical report. "What's Liver Mortis?"

"After a person dies, the blood slowly settles to the lowest portion of the body. Liver mortis is sensitive to the position of the body. Since Laura was slumped in a chair, the blood had begun to settle in her lower abdomen and legs."

I winced again. "Do we have the results of the autopsy?"

"Yes. It's definitely murder! Besides petechial hemorrhages in the whites of the eyes, the autopsy revealed that poison was injected into Laura's arm *after* she was suffocated. It was made to look like suicide."

"How could they know that the poison was injected after she died?"

"That's quite simple. Once the heart stops beating, the blood doesn't circulate. The poison injected in the arm won't travel far. In Laura's case, all the poison was localized."

A mental image ran through my mind. Somebody taking Laura's lifeless arm and trying to inject poison with a hypodermic needle. The thought turned my stomach. I had to change the subject.

"What do we know about alibis?"

Phil paced back and forth. "I found out that Paul Gerber was supposed to be in his room between 10:00 and 2:00 that night. But he doesn't have an alibi. No phone calls from his room either."

I had made discreet inquiries about Donald Armstrong. "Turns out Donald was at a corporate party from 9:00 until 2:30— a big affair on Rush Street. He went alone, but the place is a 20-minute drive to Laura's room. Some guests at the party remember talking to him. It's possible he could have slipped out during the party."

"Possible, but not likely. It rules out Professor Armstrong, though. He caught a plane from O' Hare at 9:30 Sunday night to attend a conference in Washington, D. C."

I was taken aback. Phil had actually checked out Professor Armstrong's alibi. No wonder he was a cop. They had taught him not to trust anybody.

I shifted to another topic. "Do you know what Donald Armstrong did right after he graduated from Boston College?"

"He became a partner in GO Corporation, didn't he?"

"Actually, he became a partner two years after graduation. I dug up Donald's background last night. He started his own marketing company with a friend, James Knapp from Boston. His partner was a marketing major. With Donald's psychology background, they thought they had a great combination." I went to my printer and retrieved printouts from the Internet search.

"Why is this relevant?"

"The consulting practice was hyped as a major success the first year. Donald and James were featured in *Fortune* magazine as 'young entrepreneurs most likely to succeed.' In the second year, a feud broke out between the two. James spent big bucks on a new marketing software program. Donald thought the system was a failure. He kept talking about *sunk costs*. The partnership fell apart when James wanted to spend another forty thousand dollars to fix the bugs in the program. After that, the firm was legally dissolved." I tried to piece together the information from the printouts.

"What are 'sunk costs'?" Phil wasn't sure where this conversation was going.

"*Sunk costs* are any expenditures in time, money, or effort that have been spent or 'sunk.' When making a decision, costs that are already spent should be ignored. Rather, the real question: Would you spend additional money on the project now, regardless of what was sunk before? Knapp, like most people, was trying to recoup his losses by fixing the computer program. Donald realized that the psychology of sunk costs was at work. He wasn't willing to throw good money at a bad investment."

"All right, I get the notion of sunk costs, but what has that got to do with Donald as a suspect?"

I picked up another printout. "Nothing on the face of it, except that James Knapp was involved in a hit-and-run accident two months after the consulting firm dissolved. His hip was broken. The incident made *The Boston Globe*."

Phil stopped pacing. "Are you suggesting that Donald arranged the hit and run? Even if he was angry at Knapp, that would be a risky thing to do."

"No doubt, but given Donald's ruthless and vindictive nature, I thought the accident just a few months after the feud was an interesting coincidence. That's all." Maybe I was reading too much into two events that might have been random. No point in trying to find meaning in a pattern that wasn't there.

"Digging up information about the suspects from the Internet is a good idea." Phil yawned as he picked up his coat to leave my room. "Let me see what I can find about Paul Gerber. Let's meet after class."

* * *

"Gee, Larry! Didn't you feel like punching these guys in the nose?" Chris asks impatiently.

"You mean Paul Gerber or Donald Armstrong?"

"Yes, didn't you feel like breaking their legs?"

"I was digesting Laura's loss and trying to keep my mind on the investigation. Somehow, anger hadn't become part of the equation. Phil and I had no idea what we were up against. We had to be discreet and try to get new information. We were just 'muddling through.'"

"Muddling through?"

"Muddling through is an incremental strategy—taking small, hesitant steps to solve a complicated problem. Many of us muddle through different situations. Like a meandering river tracing its course, we follow the line of least resistance. Muddling through is often due to inertia and laziness."

"If muddling through is a lazy man's approach, why were you doing it?"

"When things are evolving and there is a great deal of uncertainty, the right course of action may not be clear. In these circumstances, taking incremental steps may not be a bad idea. One giant step may lurch you in the wrong direction. Phil and I were trying to get as much information as we could. Most of the time we didn't know where to look. We weren't clear about what we were looking for either. The Internet was quite primitive back then—the search engines used to spew out a lot of junk. We probably erred by not looking for information more quickly and aggressively."

"The words 'muddling through' seem to have a negative connotation. You are saying it is not necessarily a bad thing?"

"That is right—sometimes muddling through is the rational thing to do. Consider the case of the Federal Reserve Bank or the FED as it is called. The FED can't make a definite plan and stick by it simply because business conditions are changing all the time. It has to continuously balance the risk of slower growth against the countervailing risk of higher inflation. If the FED thinks that business conditions are getting worse, it reduces interest rates to revive the economy. But if strong growth is expected to generate more demand and higher prices, the FED raises interest rates to moderate spending and cool the economy. As the FED muddles through this complicated tradeoff, it has to be nimble and to act

quickly if the need arises. When the stock market had a sudden meltdown in 1987, the FED had to provide additional liquidity immediately to prevent a more rapid drop in stock prices that may have resulted in a recession. Given the circumstances, muddling through is probably the best strategy the FED can adopt.

"So what do you do? Keep muddling through forever?"

"The FED has to muddle through on a continuous basis because the economic conditions are always changing. In most cases, once you've taken sufficient incremental steps, the alternatives and circumstances may become better defined. The time may come when one swift bold move could achieve the goal. It's all a matter of judgment and timing."

"I think I get what you are saying, Larry. Just like a ninja warrior: smooth, deliberate, and careful steps—until the time comes for one big move!" Chris chops the pillow with a swift motion of his right hand.

"That's a good analogy, Chris. Didn't they teach you something similar in Tae Kwon Do? When your opponent moves toward you, his action is already chosen, but your choices are flexible and wide open—you can respond in many different ways."

"Yes, Larry, you're right, but the timing is key. If you wait too long, you may get slaughtered. If you jump in too quickly, the rash move may open up your flank."

"Judgment about timing is a difficult skill to acquire in decision making. How long do you continue to frame an issue? When should you reframe? When should a bold move be made? The context of each situation, your own experience, and your awareness will change the answers to these questions."

"Okay! Why don't you tell me who murdered Laura?"

"I'm trying to tell you exactly how it happened, Chris. The time for one bold move had not yet come. Wait for the next move. But first, picture yourself in the slammer! You'll have to answer an important question under pressure. Let me explain how Clara did it...."

14
Negotiate and Trust or Go Bust

The trouble with the world is that the stupid
are cocksure and the intelligent are full of doubt.
—Bertrand Russell

C lara handed out a sheet of paper to the class on Thursday. She wanted to have fun in this exercise. Clara commanded attention. Her voice was sharp and crisp—a cracking whip. She adjusted her glasses and made a mock bow.

"Read the situation carefully and make the best judgment you can. Please treat this case seriously. You have twenty minutes to make up your mind."

I read the hand out:

Prisoner's Dilemma

You're in the slammer! The police have arrested you and a friend for a narcotic violation. The place is Singapore. The police have placed you and your friend in separate jail cells. You suspect your "friend" may sell you out. It really doesn't matter if you're guilty or not. You have the following four possibilities.

Scenario 1: Neither of you confess. The police probably can't prove the case. Each of you will get three years anyway.

Scenario 2: Your friend confesses, you do not. He gets one year, you'll be stuck in jail for 18 years.

Scenario 3: **You confess, your friend does not**. You get one year, your friend will be in the cell for 18 years.

Scenario 4: **Both of you confess**. Both will rot in jail for 10 years.

Think carefully! You have 20 minutes to make up your mind.

I read the handout twice. Either way the choices weren't all that great. I knew my "friend" would either confess or stay firm. Probably he would try to save his own skin.

If my friend confessed, I would get eighteen years for holding out, ten years for confessing. The choice was clear, I should confess.

If he didn't confess, I would get a year for confessing, three for holding firm. Again my advantage was to confess.

It didn't really matter what my friend did. In either case, if I confessed, I came out ahead. I made up my mind: I should confess. But wait a minute! Something was wrong. My friend was going to think exactly the way I did. His preferred strategy given the same dilemma would also be to confess. We would both end up losing big time—rotting in jail for ten years. If only I could communicate with my friend and make an agreement to hold firm. We could both get away with only three years. I tried to find my way out of the dilemma.

"Okay! Time's up!" Clara announced. "How many of you decided to confess?" Eighty percent of the students raised their hands. The other 20 percent were still trying to figure it out.

"So what will happen in this situation?" Clara asked.

Phil replied. "Cops play this game all the time. We usually separate two suspects and entice each of them to confess before the other one does. It pays for each one to confess first—that's the dominant strategy for both. The final result is that both will probably confess. Since they can't communicate, and they distrust each other, both end up getting the short end of the stick."

"Phil is right," Clara pointed out. "It's ironic that their common interest is served if both hold firm. However, from an individual point of view, it makes sense for each one to confess, given that the other person's behavior is unpredictable."

"Interesting problem," Raj Kumar said. "How does it relate to real life?"

Clara had set us up for this one. "Actually there are many situations with similar constraints. Think about election time. If either the Democratic or Republican presidential candidate were to run a clean campaign with no negative advertisements, the other candidate could win by running a smear campaign. Negative campaigns are eventually quite effective. If both candidates trusted each other, they could elevate the political discourse by running a campaign based on issues alone. This would be equivalent to both inmates holding firm. Since each wants to have an upper hand, they end up 'confessing' or running a negative campaign. A negative campaign is a loss for both the candidates and for the nation."

I looked around the classroom. Phil was busy punching the keys on his laptop. Stewart was resting his chin on the cover of his machine. Paul Gerber's face was drawn. Dark shadows circled his eyes. I wish I knew what was going on in his mind.

John Scott joined in. "Another common business example is major airlines trying to keep their fares high. If all of them could trust each other, they'd keep prices high consistently and rake in higher profits. But it pays for one airline to cut prices and attract more customers. Consequently, they all end up cutting prices and losing profits. Without implicit cooperation or trust—they shoot themselves in the foot. Explicit or implicit price agreements made by a cartel, such as the Organization of Petroleum Exporting Countries (OPEC), are not sustainable. Some members of the cartel will eventually cheat—they will sell at lower prices to gain more business. When they reduce the price to reap immediate profits, other members will chisel the price further to keep their own customers. The price cartel will eventually fall apart. Consumers benefit with lower prices."

Some students were nodding their heads. They began to see the relevance of the Prisoner's Dilemma. Clara pointed out that when one person's decisions affect another person, the sequences of choices and strategies could get quite complicated. The Prisoner's Dilemma was a well-known example of *game theory*, a sequential strategy process that analyzes the interdependence among decision makers.

Raj brought up another application. "Two people have inside knowledge about a company—let's say they have prior knowledge that the FDA is going to approve the commercial production of a new drug. Buying the company's stock based on this inside knowledge is illegal, but if they trusted each other to keep the information secret, they could probably rake in a tidy sum by buying the stock now and selling it when the price increases after the FDA press release. But they may compromise themselves or 'confess' by telling others or by buying very large amounts of the stock—actions that may alert the Securities and Exchange Commission to their criminal behavior."

Professor Armstrong paced at the back of the class. He seemed lost in thought. "How does this relate to PACE's strategy for Cicor?" he asked.

Stewart Anderson looked up from his laptop. "PACE and its major competitors, Pfizer and Merck, have to determine the amount of time they should allocate for testing the safety and effectiveness of new drugs. Time exhausted in trials is forsaken earnings, but it ensures a safer and more effective product. PACE could have a mutual pact with its competitors to spend a reasonable amount of time, say four years, for adequate testing. However, it is in the interest of each company to 'confess'— to jumpstart the commercialization of their product before others are in the market. But if they don't hold firm and spend adequate time testing their drugs, they may compromise not only the safety of patients, but also their own reputations."

"That's a good example, Stewart. Many other issues can be put in the context of a Prisoner's Dilemma." Professor Armstrong turned around. "What's the critical underpinning of the concept?" he asked.

Clara replied, "The parties are not able to sustain an agreement by either cooperation or by an effective monitoring system. All parties could win by either cooperating with each other or conforming to a sustainable agreement. But each party has an inherent tendency to look after its own interest rather than the collective well-being. It's not surprising that the final result is a bad situation for all. The mantra should be: Negotiate and trust or go bust!"

After class, Paul Gerber walked over to me. He avoided my eyes as he spoke. "Laura's death has been a shock to us all. I'm sorry it turned out this way."

I tried to gauge his emotional state from his behavior. His voice was flat—no underlying tremor or sentiment. He shifted his weight on the balls of his feet. His tired eyes indicated that he was sleep deprived.

"Thanks for your thoughts," I responded, not knowing what to think.

* * *

Phil signaled that we should walk over to the campus apartments. As we quickened our pace, he took out the *Chicago Tribune* from his briefcase.

"Have you seen today's paper?" Phil handed me the news item on page three.

ANOTHER MISHAP IN THE ARMSTRONG FAMILY
by Michael Wood
Tribune staff reporter

A hit-and-run incident was reported in the downtown loop yesterday. A business executive, Donald Armstrong, was crossing the street to the Board of Trade office on La Salle Street when a car almost hit him.

Armstrong, Vice President of *Global Options, Inc.*, was able to scramble to safety by jumping off the road just in time. He was visibly shaken after the incident. He didn't suffer any significant injury with the exception of minor bruises. The unmarked car accelerated toward him at a sudden speed of 55 miles per hour.

Phil interrupted my reading. "I was skeptical about the link you made last night between Donald and the hit-and-run incident with James Knapp," he said. "This news makes me wonder. We don't know the motive of the driver. It could be a simple case of hit-and-run by a drunken driver. But two hit-and-run accidents involving Donald is an unusual coincidence, don't you think?"

"Let me read the rest of the story," I said as I glanced at the last two paragraphs.

Two witnesses questioned by the police identified the car as a blue, mid-sized sedan. The driver of the car drove away without stopping. Police have been called in to investigate the matter. No information is available about the driver.

Armstrong's younger sister, Laura Armstrong, was found dead in her university apartment three days ago. The private funeral for Laura is scheduled for Thursday. Donald Armstrong didn't return any phone calls today. A spokesperson from *Global Options, Inc.*, condemned the incident. Anyone who has any knowledge of the event should call the police department at 312-258-2100.

I turned to Phil as I finished reading. "The two hit-and-run incidents are not similar—in this incident Donald is the victim. Besides, we shouldn't underestimate the role of chance. It could be a random streak. There are other explanations: somebody could be trying to knock off Donald. Another possibility is more intriguing. Donald could have staged this incident to throw the investigation off track, assuming he somehow knows that it's a murder case now."

"You're right. There are several explanations. What's the likelihood of each possibility?" Phil took out a piece of paper from his pocket.

I tried to be objective. "It might seem that hit-and-run events are common. Newspapers typically sensationalize these events on a slow news day. Remember the 'availability bias.' We tend to think that an event is more likely to happen if more instances can be recalled. We should look at the base rate probabilities. What are the chances of a person living in Chicago being run off the road like that?"

Phil glanced at the paper in his hand: "I'm one step ahead of you this time. During last year, two hundred and fifty incidents of hit and run were reported in the city of Chicago. Police investigators who monitor crime data believe that actual incidents are at least twice that number—many cases aren't reported. Anyway, the city's population is close to three million. Given these numbers, there's a one-in-six-thousand chance that any person in Chicago might encounter a hit-and-run incident in a year."

"Interesting stuff! I guess being run over by a hit-and-run driver is not that common after all. It does leave the other possibilities wide open."

Phil took out another paper from his jacket. "I made a search for Paul Gerber on the Net. It's amazing what a good search engine can toss up."

"A good search engine plus the right key words. What about Paul?"

"Paul made the news another time after high school. He was caught up in a pump-and-dump scandal."

"What exactly do you pump and dump?"

Phil looked at his note. "For stocks that aren't traded frequently, someone can try to manipulate their price. For instance, you could spread fictitious rumors in chat rooms and other places on the Net about why the stock is a good buy. That's pumping the stock. You buy a large portion of the penny stock before you pump it. This will increase the price of the stock and validate all the gossip. Other people will buy the stock as the rumors multiply on the Web. Once the stock has reached a high price, you can dump your stock and walk away with a nice bundle. The key is to be persuasive and target a stock that has few trades so that you can manipulate its price."

"How did Paul fit into this scheme?"

"Paul was featured in *Business Week* as a boy wonder. A nineteen-year-old kid had manipulated the market for a penny stock, Bodyworks, Inc. He walked away with forty-nine thousand dollars. The Securities and Exchange Commission came after him. There was a controversy about the ethics of the pump-and-dump strategy. It was difficult for the SEC to hold him accountable."

"I can see how that would be difficult." I recalled Raj Kumar's discussion about cause and effect. "The SEC would have to demonstrate that his actions directly contributed to the rise and fall in the stock price. Many factors can influence the stock price—other buyers, changes in the business environment, new information about the company, and random events. Besides, the veracity of his rumors had to be disproved."

"You're right about that. The causal link between his trades and the price of the stock was a major part of the controversy. Some argued that the cause and effect was not proven beyond a reasonable doubt. Others contended that those who bought the stock based on his rumors acted foolishly. The SEC dropped the case when Paul agreed to surrender thirty-five thousand dollars. He still walked away with fourteen thousand dollars and no official sanction of his conduct. In fact, he became a hero in some investment circles." Phil put the paper back into his pocket.

"The incident may have given him a false sense of confidence about beating the system," I said.

As we approached the campus apartments, Phil changed the subject: "We know Angela might be hiding something. Let's talk to her again. We're running out of time. Once the police department announces a formal murder investigation, Shawn won't be able to give us much latitude."

We located Angela as she was getting cleaning supplies from the main floor. I could sense her discomfort as we approached. Was her discomfort because of a treatment effect? The very fact that we were approaching her the second time might make her more nervous.

"Hi, Angela," Phil tried to sound informal. "We were just checking out the building again. How are you doing today?"

"Okay! I have too much work."

"I think you should know that the police are treating Laura's death as a murder, not a suicide." Phil glanced around and lowered his voice. "But keep that information to yourself. If you help us now by telling us anything you know, you won't have anything to worry about. We can make sure that you won't get into trouble. Later on, though, once the big cops start asking questions, it might be too late." Phil spread his arms wide to impersonate a big cop's stance.

Angela was irritated. "I told you before what I know. I do not know anything else. You have no right to bother me. I will call a lawyer."

"No need for lawyers," Phil soothed her. "We're talking informally, giving you some advice. Speaking of lawyers, though, do you know anyone who needs to get a green card? I know a lawyer who can arrange it very quickly."

Angela didn't respond. She twisted the end of her apron with two fingers. Phil's voice was a confidential whisper. "Help us out. We help each other. Okay? Please call me by 9:00 tomorrow. Here's my card. Don't delay. Remember, the big cops, those guys are bad! Take care. Bye now."

Angela appeared to calm down. She stopped twisting her apron. "Good-bye. I told you everything that I know."

As we walked back, Phil's step had become jaunty. "Why didn't you confront her with the fact that she lied about Sunday?" I asked, trying to figure out his angle.

"Gravitate to your own risk taste," Phil chuckled.

"What?"

"I could confront her about Sunday evening, but it would probably make her more defensive. Remember—when we try to impose safety, some people tend to take more risks in other ways. The reverse is also true: When we've somehow incurred more risk than we actually want, we look around for more safety. In general, depending on personality, people gravitate to their underlying risk taste. I think Angela has a tussle going on. She's exposed herself to more risk than she's able to handle. I threw her a lifeline. She might grab it. The fear of the big cops might help!"

I was beginning to admire Phil's manipulative skills. "Smart move. Might not work though."

"We'll have to wait and see. Where do we go from here? Any suggestions?"

We had arrived at my apartment. "I have a suggestion, but I'm not sure you're going to like it."

15
WARS that Resolve

*If decisions were a choice between alternatives,
decisions would come easy.
Decisions are the selection and formulation of alternatives.*
—Kenneth Burke

I explained my suggestion as we entered my room. "Professor Armstrong's mantra about making a decision involves three inter-connected steps: *deliberate, investigate, and evaluate.* The process of deliberation, investigation, and evaluation forms a continuous cycle—we need to do all three as we work toward a solution. We've been discussing and investigating many different aspects of the case. Now it's time for another major evaluation. We should organize our thoughts and figure out where we are at this point. How about another decision-making exercise?"

Phil grunted. "I guess it can't hurt. The last one we did on suicide or murder cleared our thinking. I haven't read this part of my class notes. Why don't you lead and write it out as we go along?"

"Let's do it differently this time. The alternative choices will be our suspects. Each suspect has different factors or attributes—like motive or opportunity. We can use numbers to weigh the importance of each attribute and a rating score to evaluate its performance. The weight captures importance. The score assesses performance. The method is called *WARS: Weighing Attributes and Rating Scores.*"

"I'm not sure I understand what you're saying, but you can explain as we go along," Phil said.

I scratched my chin. Phil's habit was rubbing off on me! "Two issues are crucial right at the outset. First, we have to figure out the importance or weight we assign to each attribute. Second, we have to decide the suspects who should be a part of the exercise."

Phil thought as he paced. "Let's consider the importance of each attribute. I think motive is very important. In my experience, motive turns out to be a critical attribute. Let's give motive a weight of five out of five."

"I agree. What about opportunity? That's important, too. What good is a motive without the time and place to do it? It's probably less than motive, though. Can we settle on a weight of four out of five?"

"That works for me. Another attribute we should consider is personality type. We have some knowledge about the personalities of the suspects. What importance would you assign to personality?"

"How about a weight of four?"

Phil made a face. "I wouldn't weigh personality that high. People can be deceiving. Who knows what's going on in their heads? We can only conjecture. I'd recommend a weight of one."

We were at an impasse on this one. "How about a weight of two as a compromise?"

Phil stopped pacing. "I'll settle for two. As far as clues about each individual are concerned, we have roughly one clue for each. Again, most clues can be deceiving. Let's allocate a weight of two for the clue we know about each suspect."

"That's fine with me."

"Okay—for attributes we have motive, opportunity, personality, and clues," Phil said. "Now, the second question: Which suspects should be on our radar screen?"

"The obvious two are Paul Gerber and Donald Armstrong. Do you have anyone else in mind?"

"Yes." Phil turned around and looked directly at me. "I don't think we should rule out Professor Armstrong. I may be behind in my readings, but I remember the principle about framing— don't draw narrow boundaries. I know how you admire Professor Armstrong, but don't let your emotions get in the way of logical thinking!"

I shrugged my shoulders. How could one argue in favor of narrow boundaries? One rationale could be to keep things simple, but as it was, we didn't have a large number of suspects. I realized that this argument would be difficult to win. Professor Armstrong would score low in all the attributes anyway.

"Okay," I said. "You win—I'll try to suspend my emotions. How about Angela? Shouldn't she be a suspect? We think she's hiding something."

"Angela is uncomfortable about something. But I don't think she has a motive. She's more likely to be an accomplice. If you don't mind, let's keep her out for the time being."

I didn't see why Angela should be excluded and Professor Armstrong included. I would have kept both out, but I didn't want to fight this battle. I wrote the three suspects as the alternatives. For each of the attributes I assigned the weights we'd agreed upon.

Phil started rubbing his hands. "All right. Shall we score each attribute for our suspects? Let's start with Paul Gerber. His motive isn't that strong. He was angry with Laura and could have exploded on the spot. Can we go with a five out of ten?"

I nodded. For opportunity we decided to give him a nine. He had no credible alibi. For personality, given his shady ethics with the pump-and-dump scandal, we settled on a seven. His clue was his prior assault during high school, and we agreed on a six for this particular clue.

I pointed to the table. "Phil, the next step is to multiply each weight with the score for each attribute. It should be clear now why we split the weight and score. The weight determines the importance of each attribute. The score captures how that attribute is evaluated for a suspect. Remember: weight for importance, score for assessment."

"I understand what you're trying to tell me. If we combine the weight and score, we're mixing importance and assessment. Motive is important, so it will always have a weight of five. Some people might have a lower assessment on motive. Keeping importance and assessment separate is a good idea. It complicates the table, but it's worth it."

The grand total of the weights multiplied by the scores for Paul Gerber worked out to eighty-seven. We moved to Donald. He scored high on motive—nine out of ten—he would be the sole heir of the fortune and he had quarreled with Laura just before her death. On opportunity, since he could have made it to Laura's room by sneaking out of the party, we gave him a three out of ten. And as for Donald's personality, both Phil and I didn't have a charitable view about his conniving. We agreed on an eight out of ten. For his clue—the two hit-and-run accidents—we settled on a five. Eventually, after multiplying his weight with the scores, we arrived at a grand total of eighty-three for Donald.

For Professor Armstrong we haggled for a while. We weren't clear about his motive. If all the Armstrong children were dead, the money would go to the charitable Armstrong Fund. I wanted a zero for motive, but Phil argued that since Professor Armstrong's motive was not clear, we should give him a five as a default. We finally settled on two. As for opportunity, Professor Armstrong caught the 9:30 p.m. flight from O' Hare, so his alibi was quite solid. We agreed on a one for opportunity.

Another battle ensued about personality. Phil thought personalities could always be deceiving; he wanted at least a five. Given that Professor Armstrong contributed to charity, we compromised with a score of three. Phil pointed out that Professor Armstrong's individual clue was the change in his behavior. He appeared to be more distracted than usual, morose at times. I thought, of course his behavior has changed. He lost his niece! But Phil was unyielding. We ended up with a six. In spite of all the arguments Phil made, Professor Armstrong ended up with a grand total of thirty-two.

When we had finished, Phil looked at the table. It had taken us more than an hour to complete.

"What have we accomplished?" he asked skeptically.

"At the very least, we were forced to think about all the attributes and evaluate their importance. We assessed each person's profile in a systematic manner. If we'd talked about the suspects without the framework, we could have gone around in circles. We were forced to confront each attribute for each of the suspects and assess it. Nothing can substitute for the wisdom needed to make good judgments, but this process provides a framework. That's all!"

WEIGHING ATTRIBUTES and RATING SCORES (WARS)

Alternatives Attributes/ factors	PAUL GERBER Score/ weightxscore	DONALD ARMSTRONG Score/ weightxscore	PROF. ARMSTRONG Score/ weightxscore
1. MOTIVE Weight: 5	5 /5x5 = 25	9 /5x9 = 45	2 /5x2 = 10
2. OPPORTUNITY Weight: 4	9 /4x9 = 36	3 /4x3 = 12	1 /4x1 = 4
3. PERSONALITY Weight: 2	7 /2x7 = 14	8 /2x8 = 16	3 /2x3 = 6
4. INDIVIDUAL CLUE Weight: 2	6 /2x6 = 12	5 /2x5 = 10	6 /2x6 = 12
TOTAL SCORE	87	83	32

Phil gave in a little. "True—the framework is simple. I can see that it could work for a lot of decisions, particularly if a business organization needs to develop a consensus on a complex issue. If executives are trying to decide which project to implement, they can list the attributes of the alternative projects—debate about the weights and scores for each attribute. The exercise provides a general frame of reference, no doubt. But look at the difference between Paul, who has a total score of eighty-seven, and Donald, with eighty-three. That's a virtual dead heat. If we shift a weight here, change a score there, Donald might come out ahead!"

I realized I was too defensive. "I agree that we shouldn't place too much importance on a slightly higher total score for Paul. We've made some implicit assumptions, and those assumptions might not hold water."

Phil looked at the table again. "I can think of a few assumptions we made. We drew boundaries around the problem. There could be a suspect out there we haven't considered. What we call clues are really specific incidents about our suspects. We could have left out some other clues. Our list of attributes could be incomplete."

"You're right. We also scored these attributes based on our *present* knowledge about each suspect. As we obtain more information, the evaluations could change. We may decide to add a new attribute or revise a score."

"Come to think about it," said Phil, "we can view some of these limitations as opportunities. This exercise can help us identify gaps in our knowledge. We can gather more information and re-work the table. In a group environment, this process could be quite useful." Phil tried to look at the bright side.

"There's no doubt we have gaps in our knowledge. We need to work more on the motive angle and be sure about the alibis. Angela is holding out on some information. We need to find out what she knows. One critical piece could throw a monkey wrench into our calculations."

My laptop light blinked. You have mail! I clicked on my e-mail icon. A message popped out:

DONALD ARMSTRONG IS SETTING YOU UP! THE HIT-AND-RUN ACCIDENT WAS A FAKE!

PROFESSOR ARMSTRONG DOES NOT APPEAR TO BE MOURNING LAURA'S DEATH.

APPEARANCES CAN BE DECEPTIVE!

A FRIEND.
PEEPING TOM

Phil looked at the laptop screen. "Our friend is active again. What are his motives? He seems to know what we're up to."

"This guy was right about Paul Gerber's past. He also knew about the murder before anyone else. Someone from the inside is trying to point us in the right direction."

Phil was on his feet. "Or he could be trying to throw us off the track. Who knows? What he's saying in this e-mail is difficult to verify. I bet we won't be able to trace this message either, but I'll try anyway. We have to get whatever information we can from Angela."

"Phil, there's something else we've been overlooking in terms of feedback. I thought about this a while ago, but I haven't followed up. By focusing only on the background information that's made the news or is available on the Net, we may be missing some critical feedback. What about relevant information that didn't make the news? We should try to find out more about the suspects from other sources. Maybe we need to inquire discreetly among our friends. Overlooking some critical feedback from less obvious sources can result in a frame with narrow boundaries."

"You're right about that Larry. Why don't you try to find out more about Donald? I'll try to get more information about Paul."

"What else can I do to help, Phil?"

"Shawn Douglas has asked for an update. Can you drive with me to his office in the evening?" Phil was punching the keys of his cell phone.

* * *

Chris starts prowling the room again with his restless moves. "Gee, Larry! How long is the story going to last? Why don't you just tell the murder story?"

"I want to give you a general sense of how to construct a grid for solving any problem. The basic idea is simple—list your alternatives in different columns, specify the attributes of each alternative in the rows. You can do it without weights if you want to simplify it, but weights allow you to account for the importance of each attribute. Multiply the weights by the scores and add up the total for each alternative. That's not so difficult, is it?"

"Well, it's a cake walk compared to algebra and trig—you're talking to a math jock here. You guys were still in the preliminary part of the decision process, weren't you?"

"That's right. We'd worked out the initial scores for each suspect and decided some of the issues. The process allowed us to identify the areas where we needed more information. Decision making is a process, and we have to keep resolving some issues and going back for more information on others. This deliberation and gathering of more information as we proceed is at the heart of the process. Remember Professor Armstrong's mantra: Track and listen to the feedback. We have to be open to criticism and aggressive about seeking new information."

"I think I know who committed the murder. Donald Armstrong is too obvious. It's Paul Gerber, isn't it?" Chris tries to do an end run.

"Well, maybe! We're not there yet. We had to figure out our game plan—the case took some unexpected turns."

Chris realizes I control the cards. "All right, Larry! What happened next? Did you guys finally nail the murderer? I can't wait. Let's move on. I'm famished. Can we call for a pizza?"

"Sure, Chris, while we're waiting for the pizza we might as well move on. Decision making is not a cold, calculated exercise—it is a hot cognitive process. We have to be aware of all the emotional baggage we bring to a decision. We need a capacity to reflect on the way we make our choices and follow through with our actions—a capacity to perceive our faults—to grapple with our fears and misperceptions. Many decisions we make can tell a lot about ourselves—dark places in our psyche we haven't mustered enough courage to explore. It's not easy to shine a bright light into the deep caverns of our mind."

"How can we do that?"

"There's no easy answer, Chris. It's something I have struggled with all my life. Two things can help. One: don't get defensive about your mistakes. Enjoy some self-deprecating humor about your own frailties. Two: try to learn from your past behavior. Many aspects of the human dilemma are at play. Can we have a larger sense of awareness about ourselves? Do means justify the ends? How should we use our intuition? I'm getting way ahead of myself. "

"Did you ever find out what Angela was holding back?"

"That was one major question confronting us. We had to try to get the information from Angela. How to do it wasn't clear. But things were about to spiral out of control—Shawn Douglas had to be brought into the picture. We had to move quickly...."

16
Tamper with the Anchor

*The real voyage of discovery consists not in seeking
new landscapes, but in having new eyes.*
—Marcel Proust

Phil was driving to Shawn Douglas's office on Thursday afternoon. "I suppose you don't want to tell me why you didn't go
to Laura's funeral today?" he prodded gently.

"Your supposition is correct," I said curtly. I was surprised
that Phil had brought up the subject again. "I need to grieve in
private, Phil. I haven't had time to do that yet. We've been running
around trying to get more information. Besides, I'd rather be in
Shawn's office trying to catch the murderer than in the middle of
a funeral ceremony. I need time to digest my loss. Is that too difficult to understand?"

"No, I realize we all grieve in different ways. I didn't mean to
pry."

I took a deep breath. "You're not prying, Phil. I don't know
what I would have done without your help. I'm sure wherever
Laura is, she's proud of you."

A thick lump constricted my throat. I sensed that Phil was trying to control his voice. I made a clumsy effort at changing the
subject.

"I found out about Paul Gerber's Cocktail Hour club. The
information was hard to get. I had to make many discreet inquiries
and wait for feedback. Turns out Paul belongs to an exclusive
society that has something to do with special cocktails."

"Cocktails that you drink?" Phil asked.

"I guess you could say that. The cocktails are deadly combinations of chemicals that can help in pain control and mercy killing. They call themselves the Cocktail Hour, but they have an agenda. The Hemlock Society considers the club's methods for euthanasia too blatant and extreme. Paul's group believes that if a person is suffering and thinks that the situation is hopeless, the person can have a lethal cocktail in their chosen last hour. The group prescribes few safeguards—no second opinions or waiting periods. They have secret access to lethal cocktails by an underground network."

"Paul Gerber, then, had access to different types of chemicals," Phil said. "After she was choked, Laura was injected with a cocktail that included sodium pentothal. Kind of points the finger at Paul, don't you think?"

"It's one additional clue, Phil. Hardly conclusive though. If he were the culprit, why would he boast about the Cocktail Hour to Laura and Clara? Besides, anyone can get sodium pentothal and other chemicals from different sources. It's surprising what can be bought on the Net—and elsewhere—if you're willing to pay the right price."

Phil switched to a different subject. "Shawn wants to talk to us about what we've discovered so far. Our informal snooping days are almost over. The police department will issue a press release soon about the autopsy. A murder in the Armstrong family is big news. The reporters will be all over the place. Shawn is going to take over the investigation and set up his team."

"We have some suspects, but no smoking gun. What can we do to jolt the case to a quick resolution?"

As Phil and I entered Shawn Douglas's office, we noticed that the pace of activity had picked up. Two police officers sorted through files, and another officer was giving directions on the phone. Shawn came out of his office to meet us.

"I'm glad you came out to help us, Larry," he said, pumping my hand. "Phil has been telling me what a big help you've been. Rather than start from scratch, I thought you guys could fill me in on what you know."

Phil took out the table of suspects we'd worked on. He had an impish grin.

"Shawn, all that we know is in this table. We'll explain the score for each suspect."

Shawn glanced at the sheet of paper in Phil's hand and furrowed his eyebrows. "Don't give me a class in mathematics. I flunked high school algebra. Just give me the lowdown in plain talk. I don't need a messy chart."

Phil's impish grin had become a smile. "This is plain talk! Let us explain what we know about each suspect. It won't take more than fifteen minutes."

Actually, it took half an hour. We explained the decision exercise and pointed out our suspicions about Angela and the e-mail messages from Peeping Tom.

Shawn took quick notes as he assessed the situation. "A lot has been going on under the surface. I don't know how this Peeping Tom guy fits in. Then there's Angela. She's probably afraid of something."

"We're almost out of time, aren't we?" Phil asked.

Shawn sat down behind his desk and propped his feet on the table. "We may be able to delay the press hounds for about twenty-four hours. Some of them are already sniffing around. If we declare any of these guys as suspects, the walls will go up. They'll want their lawyers and we won't be able to question them informally. The whole investigation will become a different ball game. Do you have any suggestions about how we could speed up the process?"

Phil rose from his chair. "I've been thinking about different ways to pry some information from Angela. We've tried a carrot and stick approach. It hasn't worked so far. What if we bring her in and try to make a deal with her?"

Shawn didn't seem to like the idea. "What kind of a deal? We don't even know what crime, if any, she's committed?"

"Humor me for a second, Shawn. Larry, I was thinking about the Prisoner's Dilemma. We can set up a situation that encourages Angela to confess."

I wasn't sure where Phil was going. "The Prisoner's Dilemma is about two suspects. It creates incentives for each of them to confess first. But Angela is only one person. How would that work?"

Shawn became more interested. "Go on!" he nodded at Phil.

"We think Angela is probably an accomplice, but we don't know for sure. It's unlikely that she murdered Laura all by herself. Angela probably knows there's another person involved. Why don't we pretend we have two suspects in custody? Angela doesn't have to know what we don't know! Let's pretend we're interviewing another person besides her. She may decide to talk rather than face the consequences if she thinks her accomplice is about to confess. We can set it up as a Prisoner's Dilemma."

Phil had a good point. I nodded to Shawn. "We've nothing to lose at this point. Just bringing her in may unnerve her. We can give her a stark choice: Cooperate and trust or go bust. Let's try to do it informally. Phil and I can pick her up."

Shawn grunted. "Make it quick. Let's hope she doesn't ask for a lawyer."

Bringing Angela to the police station took almost two hours. She was quiet on the way to the station. Phil walked Angela into the interrogation room right away. The center of the room had a small table surrounded by three chairs. Shawn and I sat in an adjacent room, looking through a one-way mirror.

"Please sit down," he told Angela. "Do you want some coffee?"

Angela was fidgeting, twisting the end of her dress with one hand. "No coffee, thank you. I need to get back to work."

Phil sat down in front of her. His face was grave. "I need to talk to you about a new development. We have a suspect in custody. My boss, Shawn Douglas, is offering the suspect a plea bargain. It's a very good offer. Shawn is talking to the suspect right now. If the suspect agrees to the plea bargain, it's over! You'll be indicted as an accomplice for murder! I have convinced Shawn to give you the same generous offer. But you have to cooperate with us—now!" Phil's voice had a hard edge to it.

Angela was holding her head in her hands. She started rocking back and forth. "I do not know. I know nothing," she said.

Phil's face was very close to her. His words exploded as rapid-fire bullets. "You do know something. You were there Sunday night! We have witnesses that put you in the dorms on Sunday. You lied to us, Angela. You're hiding something. Talk to us. We'll make sure no harm comes to you. We'll look after your interests. You have to trust us!"

Angela stopped rocking. Her upper lip trembled. "My daughter in Guadalajara has no one! I do not want to get into trouble."

"Tell us what you know. We'll try to help you. Do it now before time runs out!"

Shawn knocked and came into the interrogation room, "Our suspect next door is going to talk about Laura's case. We've called the district attorney's office to work out a plea bargain. Looks like the case may close in a few hours." He glanced at Angela.

Phil stood up. "I think we're wasting our time on this one. She doesn't know how to look after her own interests." He began to walk away.

"Wait! Wait! Do not go." Angela was sobbing. "I will talk to you! Promise me you will help me?"

Phil sat down. His words were calm and soothing. "We'll help, Angela. Take a deep breath. Tell us what you know."

Angela wiped her tears. "I know I should not have done it. But I had no choice. He told me he would report me to the immigration service. I wanted to help my daughter in Guadalajara."

"Just tell us what you know. We'll try to protect you," Phil said in a calm voice.

"I got a phone call that Sunday afternoon around 3:00. He said he would give me fifty thousand dollars if I did a small thing for him. He said he would contact a lawyer to get me a green card."

"What did he want you to do?"

"He said he would call again around 6:30. The call came just before 7:00. He asked me to go into Laura's room after she was dead. I swear she was dead already!"

"What did he want you to do?"

"He wanted me to warm her body with an electric blanket and roll her over on the bed." Angela was beginning to gain her composure.

"The police found Laura sitting in a chair. Did you go into the room again?" Phil asked.

Angela nodded. "He told me to go to the room again at 11:00. He wanted me to prop Laura's dead body in a chair and place the needle in her hand. I could not put the needle in her hand. It kept dropping from her fingers!"

"What more did he want you to do?"

Angela started sobbing again. "He asked me to make the room look normal—and to wipe everything with a cloth. I put the electric blanket in the closet next to the shoes. That is all! I did not kill that girl. Help me, please!"

Phil put a hand on her shoulder. "You don't have to be afraid, Angela. We understand you didn't kill Laura. Tell us who called you?"

Angela jerked her head to the side. "I do not know who called me. I do not know how he got my phone number."

Phil's voice was deep and even. "Did you recognize the voice on the phone? Did it sound like a voice you've heard before?"

"I could not tell from the voice. It was thick—it sounded like the voice of a robot. He said if everything went well, he would mail fifty thousand dollars to me in three weeks. I have no money. I do not want to go to jail," Angela pleaded.

"You did the right thing by telling us, Angela. Somebody tried to use you. We'll take care of you. Don't worry." Phil led her out of the room.

Phil and I drove back to campus. "Our hunch was right. Angela was hiding something. Apparently, someone spoke to her with a voice transformer. I bet the call was made from a public phone booth. Now, we're back to square one." His voice sounded deflated.

"Not quite. It's true that we don't know who called. But someone wanted to mess up the time of death. That's why he wanted Angela to warm the body with an electric blanket and shift Laura's position."

"No doubt about that," Phil agreed. "The medical report based the time of death on the body temperature and the way the blood settled. Both those readings were thrown off track by what Angela did."

Something was ringing in my head. "Weigh the anchor without rancor," I blurted out.

"What did you say?" Phil glanced at me with concern.

"The time of death has been an anchor for us. We checked the alibis on the premise that the death occurred between 10:00 at night and 2:00 in the morning. Now we know that she was dead at least three hours earlier—by 7:00. Our entire decision-making exercise has been thrown out of gear. We'll have to check what the suspects were doing between 5:00 and 9:00 Sunday evening."

"You're right! That one piece of crucial information anchored our whole decision. Now we know that information was wrong. I take it back. We're not back to square one. We've moved forward— another illusion has been torn down."

"Our decisions about each suspect were contingent on some key factors. But a decision may change when some critical variables are altered. The murderer knew that police investigations are based on the time of death. He enlisted Angela's help to change a crucial variable and to make it look like suicide."

"Professor Armstrong always warns us that decisions can be unstable—the fragility of decisions, he calls it." Phil imitated Professor Armstrong's sonorous tone: "It's important to evaluate whether our decision is robust by performing *sensitivity analysis.* A good business process always evaluates how sensitive the decision is to some key factors by constructing different scenarios." Phil sighed, "Any of the important factors could have changed and that would have altered our total scores. But we didn't know what might change, did we?"

"You are right," I said. "Any piece of information that was in our frame could change. The weights of each attribute could be altered. And even now, another critical attribute could be wrong. Sensitivity analysis is difficult because we don't know beforehand what we should change to verify the robustness of the decision."

"No doubt—there's no clear road map to check for robustness. Sometimes a particular factor may be unreliable. For instance, in marketing analysis, we might know that the projections for growth in the client base are soft. In that case, we can sketch multiple scenarios based on different projections and evaluate how that would change expected profits. But in our case, we assumed that the time of death was correct because we had no reason to doubt the medical report. I guess we should always double check the reliability of critical information and assess how *changes* in that information will influence the final decision. Anyway, let's check out the alibis of our suspects for Sunday evening between 5:00 and 9:00."

Phil was already calling his phone.

* * *

On Thursday evening, I got an unexpected call from Paul Gerber. "Larry, what are you trying to do behind my back?" he asked abruptly.

"What are you talking about Paul?"

"Meet me in the school library at 6:00. I will tell you what I mean." There was a click as he disconnected the phone without waiting for my answer.

I walked over to the library at 6:00. Paul was not around, but Stewart Anderson was showing a presentation to Clara and Raj on his laptop.

"Please join us, Larry," Stewart said. "I am rehearsing for my PowerPoint presentation about Scenario Strategies. Clara and Raj are helping out."

I nodded, still looking around for Paul Gerber. Stewart powered up his laptop. "Developing *Scenario Strategies* is a flexible way to handle an uncertain future. There are five stages for charting scenarios." Stewart brought up a slide on his laptop.

Five Steps for Robust Scenario Strategies

- Determine precise objectives, major players, and appropriate time frame.

- Identify key uncertainties, driving forces, and trigger events.

- Generate divergent scenarios based on key uncertainties and driving forces.

- Focus on the conditions you can change to generate a successful, robust scenario.

- Monitor the scenario by repeating the exercise with the latest information.

"How do you construct scenarios for the PACE case?" Clara asked.

Stewart smiled, "You have anticipated my next slide. Here is how the executives at PACE may start the process."

Objective: Maximize profits and ensure new drug doesn't pose any health hazards
Major players: Likely competitors, patients, doctors, pharmacists, and the FDA
Timeframe: The testing period and the effective life of the patent: fifteen years

---

Suddenly, I sensed Paul Gerber standing next to me. I tried to sound normal as I whispered in his ear, "Should we go outside the library to talk?"

"There is nothing these guys shouldn't hear." He responded in a loud and raspy voice. He walked away from me and stood next to Clara.

Stewart threw a questioning look at Paul as he continued. "We have already discussed the background about PACE's problem. We can identify their driving forces and critical uncertainties."

Main Driving Forces

- Amount of research dollars invested in drug testing
- Expected growth in cardiovascular disease
- Amount of time spent testing the effectiveness and safety of the drug

---

"But there are many key uncertainties in this case. How do you pick the critical ones?" Raj asked.

"That is a good question. The executives at PACE need to frame the issues in a broad context and encourage extensive feedback and discussion. Eventually, their list of key uncertainties might look like this." Stewart clicked on another slide.

Key Uncertainties

- Will all relevant information be updated and available?

- Will patients follow instructions and report problems promptly?

- Are very sick patients subject to significantly more risk?

- Will competitors react by reducing the price of their statin drugs?

I walked over to Paul and whispered in his ear again. "Well, what do you want to talk about?" Paul shook his head, but didn't reply. He looked away at a cluster of other students.

"What is the next step?" Clara asked.

"The executives at PACE have to assess how the main driving forces and the key uncertainties are expected to play out. They have to isolate the factors they can change to obtain desired outcomes. Let's say PACE decides to consider two strategic interventions that can maximize their profits: (1) a new extensive testing program for very sick patients to accurately assess their overall risk from experimental drugs and (2) a centralized database to update patient information for tracking early detection of problems. Subsequently, they can sketch out a variety of scenarios that flow from these actions. Assume they come up with four possible combinations."

Analyzing Revenue Impact of Alternative Robust Scenarios

Scenario 1: Testing of very sick patients is undertaken (Action A)
Scenario 2: A centralized updated database is constructed (Action B)
Scenario 3: Both actions A and B are implemented
Scenario 4: Both actions A and B are undertaken, but competitors reduce price by 20%

"There are so many scenarios that can be generated based on different interventions. How do the executives at PACE decide which one to pick?" Raj asked.

Stewart nodded. "They have to analyze the contingencies and the strategic implications of different scenarios. Based on their intuition and experience, they can identify a set of scenarios that are robust and that maximize profits. By robust I mean the final desired outcomes of these scenarios are less sensitive to the underlying conditions. The process can help to frame an issue from divergent viewpoints and highlight the need to monitor critical information streams. Imaginative scenarios can identify the key areas an organization needs to work on and improve for achieving desired outcomes. Scenario construction, if managed skillfully and monitored continuously, provides a flexible strategy for thriving in a dynamic environment—an environment that is difficult to specify in a formal model."

Paul had walked over to me. He burst out abruptly, "Larry, why are you asking questions about me behind my back? Who gave you the right to snoop around? If you want to find out something, why don't you ask me directly? You and your half-baked cop friend think you can do anything, don't you?"

"What exactly are you talking about, Paul?" I asked.

His crimson face was six inches from mine. "I know what you have been doing. A friend from the Cocktail Hour called me today and told me about your phone calls."

Stewart looked up from his laptop. The discomfort Raj and Clara felt was palpable. "Paul, why don't you sort this out with Larry calmly in a quiet place," Clara suggested.

"I don't need to sort anything out." Paul stabbed his finger at me. "You and your damn friend better stay out of my business!" He stomped out without another word. At that time my mind was focused on Paul—but I was about to receive new information from an entirely different source.

17
Can You Spot Your Blots?

*It has been my experience that folks
who have no vices have no virtues.*

—Abraham Lincoln

On Friday morning, I decided to find out more about Donald by calling several friends. With all the other developments, I had not gotten around to it. I wanted to make sure we were not overlooking any possible feedback. I called three people who knew Donald. Nothing noteworthy came up. The last person I called was my friend Daniel who worked at GO.

"Daniel, we haven't spoken for a while. I've had a lot keeping me busy. How have you been?"

"I'm fine Larry. Very sorry to hear about Laura. I wanted to call you after her death. Is there anything I can do to help?"

"Now that you ask, there is one thing you may be able to do for me. I'm doing some research on the Armstrong family. Some of the research is about their personal affairs. Have you noticed anything noteworthy about Donald? Since you work in the same office, I thought you might have some insight."

"What kind of information are you looking for?"

"Anything strange or noteworthy that might stick in your mind."

"This isn't a research project, is it?"

"I would really appreciate any insight, Daniel."

"You probably know all the information about Donald that I am aware of. Wait! One thing jumps out—an incident Donald had with Laura."

"What incident?"

"About three days before Laura died, she came to see Donald. They were having a heated discussion. Turns out his secretary heard part of the argument. You know how office gossip gets around."

"Do you know what the argument was about?"

Daniel sighed at the other end of the line. "I'm not sure I'm comfortable with this, Larry."

"Just give me a hint."

"The part the secretary heard was about you, Larry. Laura was arguing with Donald about you. I really don't know any details beyond that."

"I know this has been uncomfortable for you, Daniel, but I do appreciate it. Let's get together soon, okay?"

After a few more pleasantries, I put the phone down. I tried to recall the discussion about random streaks. Was I trying to find a pattern in a series of events that were essentially random? Three incidents had transpired before Laura died. First, Donald had snubbed me during the reception. Second, Laura's message on her laptop had revealed that she resented Donald's intrusion into her life. She wanted to have her own space and to make her own decisions. Third, Daniel's feedback indicated that Laura had another argument with Donald in his office—just before the murder.

The three events were linked by one common denominator: my name had come up in each incident. Was that random? These events were interconnected and they built on each other. Was this a pattern that had a distinct message? The message appeared to be that Donald and his sister did not get along. Their disagreement seemed to escalate over the three events. I couldn't assess this pattern objectively since part of their quarrel was about me. I made a note to discuss the three events with Phil. Perhaps he could provide an objective evaluation. My eyes drifted to the clock. I had to go to class in fifteen minutes.

* * *

Professor Armstrong was late for class. We waited for ten minutes. When he arrived, he appeared rushed. Without any pleasantries, he asked a question.

"Here's an acrostic sentence: **T**he **W**ise **C**an **G**ive **N**ew **D**irection **T**oday. This sentence can help you to remember the seven mantras. What are the first three concepts?"

Clara responded:

"**T**he Name of the Game is the Frame.

Weigh the anchor without rancor.

Cause and effect is hard to detect."

"Who'll recite the next three?" Professor Armstrong encouraged. Raj spoke up:

"**G**ravitate to your own risk taste.

Negotiate and trust or go bust.

Deliberate, investigate, and evaluate."

"Thank you Clara and Raj. Today, we'll talk about the last important piece: **T**rack and listen to the feedback. You've read about how decision making and feedback should be integrated as an ongoing process. We have to aggressively seek overlooked feedback and be conscious of subtle treatment effects. But feedback and monitoring are more than just getting information about decisions. We need to step back and reflect on the way we make our decisions. How do we go about examining our process?"

Raj raised his hand. "One place to start is to find out if the decision-making process we normally follow actually succeeds in achieving our objectives. Our process should ensure that we don't lose frame control."

Professor Armstrong nodded. "Anyone else?"

Clara contributed. "Another strategy could be to calibrate the decision-making process by feedback. To ensure that when we make a similar decision again, we follow a better process and are more well informed."

Phil had another angle. "We should examine the key judgments we made. We need to assess with hindsight whether or not we collected the relevant information and made the right calls. With this kind of self-examination, we can fine tune our decision-making process."

Professor Armstrong stopped pacing. "All of you are right in a way, but Phil comes closest. The key is an honest self-examination of the process you follow. There's no ideal process that will suit everyone. You have to fine tune the process based on your own strengths and weaknesses. Step outside yourself for a moment and try to be objective about the process you follow."

"What exactly are you looking for in this self-examination?" Clara asked.

"There are no specific questions that will suit everyone, Clara. You have to make up your own questions. Are you vigilant about the biases that normally seduce you? For important decisions, do you collect enough information? Are your boundaries around a frame too narrow? But don't rely on these questions alone. If you look hard enough, you'll know your own weaknesses. Track and listen to your feedback—not only about your decision, but also about the process you follow. An honest self-examination can provide valuable insight."

I looked at Paul Gerber. His eyes were bloodshot, his hair and clothes appeared rumpled. Paul's face had an opaque, expressionless look. He had not talked to me since he stomped out of the library. He avoided my glances. Phil was punching away on his laptop. I wondered what mistakes we were making in our decision-making process. I scribbled a note to Phil: *Did you check the alibi for Paul Gerber? We should audit our decision-making process.*

John Scott spoke up. "What about business organizations? We've discussed how they can fall into the trap of groupthink. What can they do to ensure a better decision-making process?"

Professor Armstrong put his right hand in his pocket. "In a corporate environment, we need to formalize a process of self-examination. Many business teams make complex decisions in an organization. Periodically, each team should examine anew their process of decision making."

"What kind of questions should they ask?" Stewart looked up from his laptop.

"Again the questions depend upon the circumstances. A corporate self-audit has to be candid and context-specific. Were the objectives well specified? Did we miss any angle when we framed the issue? Do we still rely on anchors that have become obsolete? Are we missing some critical feedback from clients? Do treatment effects contaminate our feedback? We have to actively question our presumptions, gather more relevant information, and continue to refine our strategy."

"Will following all these guidelines ensure success?" Stewart asked.

"No, but we can try to minimize the chances of failure. Clearly, even a good process can lead to bad outcomes because of many unpredictable events. The important thing is to examine the process impartially and objectively so that improvements can be made. Some corporations have saved millions of dollars based on candid decision-audits."

Raj asked, "Are these kinds of self-examinations and learning from the process common among corporations?"

"Surprisingly, most companies don't formalize a process to examine their critical decisions. They miss a great opportunity to improve future decisions. One impediment is that it may lead to finger pointing and acrimony. But it's possible to examine decisions in a non-threatening environment. A corporation can seek the help of a neutral party to examine past decisions. It should be clarified that the process won't influence performance evaluations."

Phil's scribbled note came back: *Paul Gerber was in the library until 5:00 that afternoon. He was seen in the commons at 6:00. Beyond that, we don't know.*

Professor Armstrong paused. "Let's talk about a decision audit for PACE. What are the five key lessons PACE executives can learn from our discussions? What can make them **WISER**? Each of the five lessons can be derived from the acronym WISER. What is the lesson for W?"

John Scott replied. "They need to be vigilant about developing a **W**ide frame—incorporate in their mindset the behavior, expected response, and the vulnerabilities of all the major players. If a significant number of patients die while taking a medicine for whatever reasons, PACE's safety record and credibility are questioned. If they don't develop a wide frame, they may have to pay dearly for the failure of the weakest link in the chain of events."

Raj looked up. "The role of <u>I</u>n-time information seems critical in their decision process—that is why we recommended developing a centralized database with information provided by patients, doctors, pharmacists, and the FDA. If they don't get information quickly and intervene as the problem is developing, the ultimate solution may be more costly—both in terms of money and their reputation."

"What begins with an 'S'?" Professor Armstrong prodded.

Scott responded: "Timely information is important, no doubt—but it has to be relevant and reliable. PACE has to be vigilant about <u>S</u>ample bias. We found that the FDA trials probably had a biased sample: Compared to the patients that were profiled in the trials, the patients at large were less healthy and took other drugs. The test results could be misleading because the samples were not representative of the typical patients. PACE should conduct separate trials for more sick patients. The information flow has to be timely and reliable. Otherwise, it is garbage in and garbage out."

"Good. What are the other two lessons?" Armstrong asked.

Clara had a different angle. "PACE executives need to <u>E</u>valuate the trade off between short-term objectives and long-term consequences. Pushing for higher doses of powerful drugs to increase their effectiveness, without fully understanding their long-term consequences, might result in higher short-term profits. But they need to verify if this aggressive strategy compromises their long-term reputation and shareholder value. They need to correctly evaluate their risks and rewards over a longer timeframe. Immediate short-term profits should not compromise their long-term reputation and viability."

"What is the fifth lesson?" Professor Armstrong looked around for any other volunteers. Many students were avoiding Professor Armstrong's glances. There was an uncomfortable silence. "Here is a hint, what about the uncertainties inherent in their problem. Are patients going to follow doctors' directions? How will competitors react to higher doses for a new medicine? What is the best way for PACE to grapple with the key uncertainties? What begins with 'R'?"

Stewart closed his laptop. "Constructing a variety of **R**obust scenarios may be the best way to assess the impact of key uncertainties and the main driving forces. They have to identify what factors they can control and influence to bring about successful outcomes. The projected scenarios should be robust—ensure a high likelihood of realizing the desired outcomes. They can develop an overall strategy that incorporates the behavior and vulnerabilities of patients, doctors, and pharmacists."

Professor Armstrong nodded. "Remember PACE executives can be **WISER: W**idening their frame, **I**n-time information gathering, **S**amples that are representative, **E**valuating their short- and long-term goals, and **R**obust scenario construction can all lead to a successful strategy for PACE."

I sneaked a note to Phil: *Donald left his office at 4:30 Sunday afternoon. I couldn't find out where he was after that. He went to the party at 9:00.*

Clara had a follow-up question. "I am a bit confused. We are concluding that PACE should try to pin down the key uncertainties by developing robust scenarios. What about other methods we talked about? Should PACE employ the Balance Sheet and the WARS methods?"

Professor Armstrong took a few moments to focus on the question. "I'm glad you brought up different ways to decide, Clara. Any component of a complex decision process can be broken down and analyzed with the three procedures: Balance Sheet, WARS, and Scenario Strategies. We want to be flexible in our approach. We don't want to squeeze every problem into the same decision frame. Use your judgment to adjust a decision frame to the problem. It is a good idea to **B**egin **W**ith **S**implicity. Initially use the **B**alance Sheet method, then graduate to **W**ARS and **S**cenario Strategies."

"So which method is the best for PACE?" Clara persisted.

"PACE can analyze the pros and cons of having separate trials for less healthy patients by the Balance Sheet method. It can evaluate several alternatives for constructing databases by WARS. But eventually given the dynamic uncertainty, PACE will need to construct robust scenarios that shape their overall strategy. As we progressively complicate the process of decision making, employing one method does not preclude using other procedures."

Raj raised his hand. "Begin with simplicity, and complicate the method only if the additional complexity is useful. Isn't this principle called *Occam's razor*?"

Professor Armstrong clarified. "Yes, but parsimony is desirable as long as we don't over simplify the problem. For any given model, we can always use Occam's razor to 'shave off' those concepts, variables, or constructs that are unnecessary. But in order to incorporate the major dimensions of a complex business problem, we may have to progressively employ more sophisticated methods. You can think of it as mental exercise. Initially employ the simple Balance Sheet method to build your insights and flex your muscles. Once you have sufficient understanding of a complex problem and adequate data, graduate to more vigorous exercises such as WARS or Scenario Strategies."

I was finding it difficult to focus on the discussion. Phil's note came back: *We have to meet Shawn now. Let's sneak out.* I nodded to Phil and mouthed: *You go first.* When Professor Armstrong turned to write on the white-board, Phil slipped out of class. I waited for a few minutes, and as the professor was walking to the front of the class, I made my exit.

We walked briskly toward the parking lot. Phil shook his head and looked at his watch.

"I guess there are more important things going on than our grade. I couldn't wait. It's 10:20 right now. Shawn Douglas called me before class. He can't keep the press out of this story. The district attorney's office wants to know the facts. Shawn had to schedule a press conference for tomorrow morning. If we don't make progress today, we're in a different ball game tomorrow."

"What can we do in less than a day?" The urgency was frustrating.

"I don't know. We have to figure it out. Whatever we do, it has to be done in the next few hours. We're going to Shawn's office right now. Why don't we drive together? Just leave your car here."

* * *

"Gee, Larry! I don't get you guys. You're trying to solve a murder. Time is running out. You're still attending class. Talk about priorities!" Chris

paces back and forth. His restlessness is contagious. I get up from my recliner.

"I know it sounds strange—attending class when we're running out of time. But this wasn't just any class; it was Professor Armstrong's lecture. He had wired our brains to fill every unforgiving minute with sixty seconds' worth of distance run. To cut his class was sacrilegious. The class was also helping us to solve the crime. Anyway, do you understand the need for self-evaluation? Trying to come up with a better decision-making process?"

"I remember what Professor Armstrong said on the first day of class. The most important thing is to learn from your mistakes."

"Yes, Chris, that's true. However, we can't learn unless we continue to audit our decision-making process. It all starts with an ability to look at our own behavior with a certain amount of objectivity. Can you relish finding your own mistakes? We enjoy finding other people's mistakes— why not our own?"

"I never thought about it that way, Larry, but I suppose you're right. I love to find my friends' mistakes. On the other hand, sweeping under my own bed is rough business. You need a high level of self-esteem to really like criticizing yourself, don't you?"

"Perhaps. I think it isn't necessarily self-esteem that gets in the way. It's the notion that mistakes are inherently bad. If we recognize that we're bound to make mistakes, we develop a healthier attitude. Professor Armstrong was dead on—the real mistake is not to recognize our folly and learn from it."

"What do you mean?"

"Mistakes involve a combination of things—wrong priorities, bad judgment, inadequate knowledge, and an impulse to jump to conclusions. We have to realize that information is always changing and we should always continue to learn. Look at PACE's case with Cicor. Based on our information, we were probably correct in arguing that PACE should not aggressively push for higher dosages of Cicor without understanding the long-term risks to patients. But now more recent studies have shown that lowering your bad cholesterol below one hundred, especially for patients with higher risk, can reduce the risk of a heart attack significantly. With this new information, the cost-benefit ratio has changed, but we still need to evaluate the options on a long-term basis."

"What is the point?"

"The point is that most mistakes occur because we choose impulsively based on preliminary information. If we have time, we should take the opportunity to review our decision as new information flows in. Learning from our mistakes often implies improving our judgments with better information."

"How do you improve your judgment?"

"I believe it all goes back to a general sense of awareness. We have to understand how our thinking is influenced by our emotions and our mindset. Learn effectively from valuable experience. We have all kinds of stress in our professional and personal lives. The best way to deal with this relentless pressure is to build an inner sanctuary—a place somewhere in the deep recesses of our mind—where we can escape from the daily grind of preoccupations. As an executive in a stressful job, I had to develop a quiet space within me—not only to reduce stress, but also to fully connect with and harness my own intuition and creativity. This internal odyssey is without doubt the longest journey."

"Now you're getting philosophical again, Larry! Let's get back to the story. Did you guys finally nab the murderer? I can't wait to hear what happened."

"Both Phil and I realized that we were out of time. Our discretion to snoop around was at an end. The time had come for one swift stroke. The only problem was we hadn't figured out what that move would be. We drove to police headquarters in Phil's car...."

18
The Frame is the Name of the Game

*We are continually faced by great opportunities
brilliantly disguised as insolvable problems.*
—Lee Iacocca

We drove along Harrison Street toward police headquarters. The morning rush hour had subsided, but the cold cloudy day did little to dispel our frustration. I noticed some patches of black ice on the street. Phil was flooring the gas pedal. The speedometer approached eighty miles per hour. You can't nail a cop for speeding!

"Slow down! Will you, Phil? Skidding into an oncoming car won't do us any good."

"Don't worry, I know every bump on this street," Phil said—but he eased back slightly on the gas. "Given the shift of the time between 5:00 and 9:00 on Sunday, where does it leave our suspects?"

I took out the paper with our decision model. "Since Donald doesn't seem to have an alibi, I guess we could bump up Donald's opportunity score from a three to a nine. Paul Gerber was seen around 6:00; we could drop his opportunity score from a nine to a six. Wouldn't you agree?"

Phil nodded impatiently. "I have no quarrel with that. The problem is our information about the alibis isn't precise. How does the overall score change with this new input?"

While Phil accelerated through a yellow traffic light, I looked at my calculations.

"Donald's overall score jumps up to a hundred and seven. Paul's goes down to seventy-five."

"The change in scores due to the new time anchor is quite significant. You've forgotten Professor Armstrong. He was seen at the faculty dining room at 5:30 on Sunday, then he boarded a flight from O'Hare at 9:30. He arrived at the airport early. His ticket was checked in at 8:10. We don't have any other information. I'd put at least an eight for his opportunity score." Phil honked at a slow car.

I didn't want to repeat the argument we had about Professor Armstrong's scores. "That gives him a total score of sixty."

Phil parked his car at police headquarters. "We're trying to calibrate our decision with more feedback, but our information about each suspect isn't precise. These scores could change significantly as we incorporate new information, wouldn't you agree?"

We got out of the car and walked to the building. "No doubt," I said. "We haven't incorporated Paul's affiliation with the Cocktail Hour and Donald's quarrel with Laura into the framework. These scores are a work in progress. We still haven't figured out the motives that well. Who knows what's going on in a person's head? Our knowledge about the alibis is ambiguous. Let's not fool ourselves. At this point we're guessing."

Phil pressed the elevator button. "True, the quality of the information and how we resolve some key uncertainties is critical. But the table's a good way to grapple with the process of decision making. We've narrowed our thinking to a few important variables. You know what surprises me?"

"What?"

"Here we are, sick to our stomachs about Laura's death, running around trying to solve the case. Yet we're always talking about the decision-making class—this bias and that effect. Aren't we getting into a perpetual classroom mode?"

I thought about that for a minute. "You're right, Phil, it's surprising. This decision-making stuff is contagious. So much of what we've learned can be used every day. It would have been useful to take a class like this in high school. Professor Armstrong is right—I guess we're learning to thrive on our stupidity!"

"Or stupidity is thriving on us!" Phil said as we entered Shawn's office.

Shawn Douglas was pacing up and down the length of his office. He didn't indulge in any preliminaries as Phil and I shook his hand.

"I've been walking around my office for the last hour. It's more work than I normally do on a treadmill. But I promised myself I wouldn't stop until I had a plan. I think we can find a way to speed up the process."

"Let's hear it." Phil sat down in a chair.

Shawn didn't stop moving. "We have some information that we can control—the role played by Angela and the electric blanket. I've been asking myself how we can construct a scenario to capitalize on this information." He paused.

"Go on!" Phil demanded.

"What if one of my detectives was to send an e-mail to all the suspects—to each one individually. Each will think that the message came exclusively to him." Shawn kept pacing.

"What would the e-mail say?" Phil asked.

"The detective could identify himself as a police officer and pretend to blackmail the murderer. The message could say, 'I know what you did with the electric blanket. Meet me in a public place. If you bring twenty-five thousand dollars, I'll remain quiet.' Something like that. We could smoke out the suspect." Shawn looked at us from the corner of his office.

Phil replied, "That's pretty good thinking, Shawn. Let's try to refine our scenario strategy. How would I react if I was the murderer and I got this message? I'd be shocked that someone in the police department knew about the electric blanket. Or I could ignore the message and hope for the best, or send an anonymous reply that I'll pay up later. Why tip my hand?"

Shawn realized that Phil had a point. We hadn't yet hit on the right recipe. My mind raced through recent events. Phil was right about the compensation hypothesis—people gravitate to their own comfort level of risk. Phil had tried to encourage Angela to compensate by moving toward safety. When he talked to her in the dorms, it hadn't worked. The carrot wasn't sweet enough or the stick wasn't big enough. When we brought her to police headquarters, the urgency and the threat had become more credible.

I said, "One problem with a detective sending an e-mail is that the murderer might not believe the threat. How did the detective come to know? Even if the murderer decides to pay to keep the informant quiet, he'll realize that it doesn't buy him that much security. He could be blackmailed again." I paused for effect. "What if Angela sent the e-mail? The threat is more credible. The murderer knows that Angela is involved."

Phil nodded. "I think that's an improvement. We need to create a sense of urgency. What if Angela says that the cops have been pressuring her and she's about to crack?"

Shawn's pace slowed down, "Go on! What else could we do?"

The carrot still wasn't sweet enough. How could we up the ante and sweeten the deal for the murderer? I glanced at the bulletin board in Shawn's office. A poster about a vacation trip to Cancun, Mexico, was tagged on the board. In a flash it came to me.

"What if Angela says that not only is she about to confess, but she wants to leave for Mexico tonight to escape the whole thing. She wants to be with her daughter in Guadalajara, but she has no money to make the trip."

Phil caught on right away. "That may tip the scale. Not only does the murderer remove a possible threat, he'll realize that Angela's skipping the country will make her look like a suspect! If Angela promises to leave the country and never come back, the murderer will be tempted to let Angela be the red herring!"

Shawn stopped pacing. "Now I know what they teach you guys at St. Andrews. You two are devious."

"No, we're not devious, just thriving on our stupidity," Phil said.

"Thriving on what?" Shawn was at a loss.

"Never mind. Actually, we flipped our class notes: The frame is the name of the game!"

"You've lost me again," Shawn was getting restless. "We have to move right away. Phil, do you want to take a stab at a draft?" He pointed to his computer.

Phil sat in front of Shawn's computer and typed:

> I CAN'T TAKE IT ANYMORE. THE COPS HAVE QUESTIONED
> ME TWICE.

> EACH TIME THEY MAKE MORE THREATS! THE COPS
> ARE OFFERING ME A REWARD IF I TALK. MY DAUGHTER IN
> GUADALAJARA IS SICK. I NEED TO SEE HER IMMEDIATELY.
>   IF YOU BRING $30,000 TO FERNANDO'S RESTAURANT
> ON HALSTEAD STREET TODAY, I'LL LEAVE FOR MEXICO
> TONIGHT.

Shawn read the message over Phil's shoulder. "Good so far.
We have an arrangement with Fernando's—we already have cameras in the restaurant."

Phil continued typing:

> I HAVE A MEXICAN PASSPORT. I'LL MAKE A LIFE IN A
> DIFFERENT PART OF MEXICO. THE COPS HAVE ASKED ME
> TO COME TO THE POLICE STATION TOMORROW
> MORNING. MAKE SURE YOU ARE IN FERNANDO'S
> TONIGHT AT 7:30 PM. DON'T FAIL ME.

Shawn picked up the phone and dialed Angela's number. He
talked rapidly:

"Angela, this is Shawn Douglas. We have a deal for you. We'll
recommend to the district attorney's office not to make a case
against you at all. In fact, a small reward from the police department is possible if you do us a favor. Let me ask you a very
important question. Do you have a personal computer at home
linked to the Internet?"

Angela's voice came over the speakerphone, "A computer?
Yes, I have a computer. I buy things on eBay all the time. What
kind of a deal are you talking about? What is happening? I am
frightened."

Shawn's voice was soothing. "Don't worry about anything.
We have it all figured out. Phil and Larry are coming over to
explain everything. We need to send a message from your computer within the next hour. Stay in your apartment and they'll be
there in half an hour."

Shawn turned and looked at us. "We send this message to all
three suspects individually?" he queried.

Phil looked at me. "It can't hurt. If you're not the murderer,
you'd think the message is from a crazy person anyway."

Angela was not thrilled about the idea. She didn't want to get involved.

"But you are involved!" Phil said. "If you go with our plan, the police will recommend a complete acquittal. You can make some money besides. We'll guide you every step of the way."

Angela realized that her options were limited. "One condition: no guns. Okay?"

"There'll be detectives in the restaurant with guns to protect you. They'll be disguised as customers and waiters. At some point, the murderer might get desperate. He probably won't do anything violent in the restaurant, but we have to take precautions. Trust us. We know what we're doing," Phil tried to soothe her.

Angela's shoulders slumped. "I do not have a choice, do I? I need to call my daughter now. You guys can use my computer."

* * *

It was 7:25 p.m. Shawn, Phil, and I were huddled in a van, half a block from Fernando's restaurant. Fifteen minutes earlier Angela had walked into the restaurant and sat in a booth. A TV monitor showed her fidgeting with the napkin. Another monitor revealed customers streaming into the restaurant. Angela was wired with a microphone. We could hear the noise from the diners.

The tension was mounting. Somebody had to talk to break the silence. I turned away from the monitor and looked at Phil and Shawn.

"We're making two assumptions in our scenario. One, that the murderer will take the bait. Two, he'll show up in person. What if he sends someone else?"

Phil replied, "That's possible. If someone else shows up, we can try to get him to lead us to the murderer. But the murderer may not want to involve another accomplice at this stage. We're also assuming that the murderer is one of the three suspects."

Shawn grunted. "This is our best shot. If we fail, it'll be another day and another game tomorrow."

It was 7:30 p.m. Our eyes were glued to the TV screens as new customers entered the restaurant for dinner. Some of them moved to the bar as they came in. Angela sipped a drink. Her hand trembled as she picked up the glass.

Three people walked into the restaurant. Two walked over to the bar. We looked intently at the third person. A hat was low on his face. He looked around at the seating arrangement. He walked over to Angela's table. The man slid down and sat in front of Angela. He took off his hat. The camera caught the back of his head. I let out a gasp. I knew the back of that head.

"Who is it?" Shawn exclaimed, as he heard another gasp escape my lips.

The man turned his face as he took off his jacket. His profile was plain on the monitor. There was no question about it.

The man who sat in front of Angela was Martin Armstrong! His voice was flat and firm.

"I want to make sure you leave for Mexico tonight. I'll give you twenty thousand dollars right now. Another twenty thousand will be sent to you in Mexico, if you play the game right."

I couldn't focus on the monitor anymore. Phil was looking at me.

"I'll be damned," Shawn muttered under his breath. Phil was asking me something, but my mind had gone numb.

"I'll be damned," Shawn grunted again. "Look at the fish we've caught. Can we make any sense out of this?"

19
What Means to What Ends?

There are two parts to the human dilemma.
One is the belief that the end justifies the means.
The other is the betrayal of the human spirit.
—J. Bronowski

I woke up on Saturday morning with a splitting headache. The news was all over the place. The *Chicago Tribune* headline stared at me:

NEW DEVELOPMENT IN ARMSTRONG CASE
by Thomas Walker
Tribune staff reporter

In a lightning move, Chicago police led by Chief Detective Shawn Douglas arrested Professor Martin Armstrong last night at 7:45 p.m. in Fernando's Restaurant on South Halstead Street. Details are sketchy at this point, but Detective Douglas promised a press conference today at 4:00 p.m. A spokesperson from the district attorney's office said, "We are awaiting a full brief from Chief Detective Douglas." He declined to answer further questions.

My head throbbed. I'd had a sleepless night, tossing back and forth. My mentor, Martin Armstrong, the person I admired the most, had murdered his own niece! It didn't make sense. My whole world had been thrown out of gear. A rage built up in me. I couldn't erase the picture of Laura collapsed on the table, her body cold and lifeless. My mind shifted to another picture. Martin

Armstrong suffocating Laura with a pillow. I read the next two paragraphs:

> Five days ago, Professor Armstrong's niece Laura Armstrong was found dead in her dorm apartment. Initially, the death was deemed to be a suicide. During the last two days, however, unconfirmed reports indicate that Laura Armstrong might have been murdered.
>
> Donald Armstrong, the last surviving heir to the Armstrong fortune, didn't have any comment. A spokesperson from his office indicated: "Donald is grieving for the loss of his sister. Apparently, Professor Armstrong's arrest has been another blow." Professor Armstrong and Donald are managing partners of Global Options, a consulting firm. Indications regarding motive are highly speculative at this point....

I couldn't read the paper anymore. Somewhere deep within, a part of me had died and wasted away. Laura's murder was a tragedy in itself, but this feeling was different. In one swift blow I had lost a father for the second time. The contours of my value system had lost their definition. I did not have faith in my ability to recognize the good from the bad anymore. My moral sense of order—the way things are supposed to be—was in chaotic disarray. Everything I looked at seemed different. Somehow, I had to reconstruct a new sense of reality.

The phone rang. "Feel like talking?" Phil asked.

"Not really. What's there to talk about? I'm just so angry, Phil. I don't know what to think anymore."

"Talking will make you feel better." Phil didn't give up easily.

"Let's try to meet later, Phil." I tried to sound normal. "I just need some time to recoup."

I looked at the prescription from my doctor: Prevacid®. I popped a capsule into my mouth and washed it down with a glass of milk. Mylanta was not going to work anymore.

* * *

Two days later, Phil drove me to police headquarters. Angela got an informal reward of three thousand dollars—the police department didn't want to make a big deal about it. Phil had found Angela a lawyer to get her a green card. She was likely to get a two-year suspended sentence. Shawn Douglas and his sting operation were the buzz of the town. He had singled out Detective Phillip Myers as an outstanding cop. "My boy is going to go places," he said. "I'm recommending a citation for Phil Myers."

Phil and Shawn had arranged a meeting for me with Martin Armstrong. I wasn't sure that talking with him in his cell was a good idea. I was still in shock. I did not know how to deal with my new sense of reality. I was not sure I could control the deep sense of betrayal—the hurt and the anger that had built inside me. Phil was driving slowly this time. No hurry to get there. He looked at me.

"Don't take this so hard. Try to keep a sense of perspective."

"What perspective? The one Martin Armstrong gave us?" Saying his name brought acid into my mouth. "My world doesn't make sense to me anymore, Phil."

"That's why I want you to talk to him." Phil appeared concerned. "It might bring some closure." Phil seemed to wrestle with something. "I've got a confession to make."

"What?" I asked. Phil rarely admitted anything.

"All that time, when I was arguing about the weights and scores for Armstrong, I didn't consider for one second that he was the murderer. I was trying to play all the angles, to keep my emotion out of the process. But deep down, I couldn't ignore my feelings any more than you could." Phil's face was despondent.

I sighed. "I'm more guilty about this than you are. I couldn't separate my values from my facts. Somehow my personal feelings got in the way. Look at Martin Armstrong! Does he have feelings? What kind of decision model did he use?"

"Ask him when you see him today." Phil tried to make a joke. "But you're right. We were off track partly because we didn't keep our feelings out of the analysis. Our information was not complete and reliable, either. The fact that we had to be discreet was a big handicap. There's a lesson here."

"Not the classroom mode again!"

Phil ignored my groan. "The decision-making process is a vehicle. It's not the destination. It can take us somewhere—and it did. Don't forget we cracked the case. But how we drive the vehicle is up to us. We have to navigate carefully and constantly look around for new information. Curiosity, Caution, and Clear thinking are the road signs. The three critical Cs."

Trust Phil to find a lesson in the midst of a tragic situation.

"You're right," I said. "We have to question our assumptions and be frank about our mistakes. Martin Armstrong taught us that, remember?" I couldn't resist. The irony was too much to bear.

* * *

I didn't have to knock on his door this time. The guard spoke in a loud voice as he opened the gate. "Larry Rowe is here to see you."

The cell was bare—a chair and a metal table with a stack of books stood in the center. A small bed with white sheets lined a wall. In the far corner I noticed a sink and a toilet. In the dim light, I had to look around for him. Martin stood erect, facing the long side of the decrepit room. The plaster was peeling off on each side of the room around him. His dark shirt and pants blended into the faceless wall. His shoulders were arched tight, his hands nestled deep in his pockets. He didn't turn around at the guard's voice.

"Larry, do you know how many people died of AIDS in the sub-Saharan region of Africa this year?" His voice was calm and flat. No emotion.

I tried to suppress the anger that gnawed at me. "Give me your reference list! I'll run out to the library and get you the answer. Another mind-bending exercise for a twisted mind!" I couldn't keep the resentment out of my voice.

Martin turned and looked at me. His face was haggard. Our eyes met for an instant. I sensed turmoil in his tired eyes. I looked away at the wall.

"More than two million lives were lost to AIDS in the sub-Saharan region of Africa this year. If we don't respond forcefully, in the next three years, another eight million lives may be lost in this region alone. AIDS is spreading to other parts of Africa, Asia, and Russia." His voice developed an edge to it. "How much does it take to save one life? A few hundred dollars?"

I took a deep breath. "What has that got to do with your cold-blooded murder? I don't want another lecture from you."

Martin sat down on the chair. "Why are you so unconcerned about these millions of lives lost every year? Is it because you don't know them? How do we justify letting someone with AIDS die because we don't spend a few hundred dollars?"

I shook my head. "I don't want a lecture on morality either. You used your own hands to choke the life out of Laura. She was your niece!"

"Fifteen billion dollars! That's a lot of money." Martin was looking at the wall again. "Think how many lives I could have saved! Fifteen billion dollars in the Armstrong Fund would have been under my control. I wouldn't have kept a dime—the trust fund stipulates that I can't use the money for my own benefit. But I would have been able to arrest the growth of AIDS in different parts of the world. Don't you see how the money can save lives?" At last I detected some emotion in his voice.

"What gives you the right to decide who lives and who dies?" A taste of bile surfaced in my mouth.

"No one gave me the right, yet somebody has to make a choice." His voice grew flat again. "We make decisions all the time that inevitably determine life and death. We decide not to repair an old bridge, and subsequently it collapses when a school bus goes over it. Make no mistake: We killed the students in the school bus. Every day, we weigh life and death by deciding on different trade-offs."

His logic irritated me. "Those are indirect consequences of different spending choices. Where does this kind of crazy logic end? You don't want to kill old people to support the young, do you? You don't choke your own niece based on a cost-benefit ratio!"

"Why are you not concerned about the eight million who are going to die?" he asked again.

I looked at the wall. I was tired of his intellectual games. For a long moment he just sat there, waiting for a reply. I kept looking at the wall. Two ships, drifting away from each other, continents apart. After a while, he stood up and walked to the corner of the cell. When he turned, he had a faraway look in his eyes.

"Five summers ago, I discovered a cure for my depression. I found that I could help thousands of people in the sub-Saharan region. I tasted a high that I had never experienced before. I could look into somebody's eyes and say, 'You're going to live!' I need the money to make a difference. Look at the cost-benefit ratio. Three lives weighed against millions!"

Three lives! The full realization of his words hit me. "You were planning to knock off all three Armstrong heirs, weren't you?"

Martin shook his head. "It doesn't matter now. I can't help anyone anymore." He sighed. "What happens to me is inconsequential. I signed a confession today. I have failed miserably."

I tried to put the pieces together. "You hired someone to murder both Diane and Laura during the mugging incident outside the theater! When the mugging was botched, you had to finish the job."

Another thought dawned on me: "You tried to run Donald down, or maybe you hired someone to do it. That would have completed the job. Fifteen billion dollars to get a high on!"

Martin couldn't meet my eyes. "It doesn't matter anymore," he repeated, staring at the floor.

My mind was racing. "You're Peeping Tom. You sent us those e-mails to throw us off track. Why did you criticize yourself?"

"Wouldn't help if the e-mails always criticized others, would it?"

"How did you know? How did you catch on that we knew it was murder?"

Martin rose and walked to the far side of the room. He looked at the trashcan. "I notice everything that goes on in my classroom. It's amazing what kind of papers you can find in a trashcan."

I sank down on the hard bed. How could I have been so stupid? I remembered rolling Phil's message into a paper ball during class. I had thrown the paper ball into the trashcan. Martin had pieced together our torn messages!

Another question occurred to me. "Why did you decide to use Angela to further your plans?"

Martin walked back to the chair. "Three years ago I was in Mexico during the summer. I spent four weeks in Guadalajara— I was there when Angela's daughter was born. Her daughter has some developmental problems."

"Why did you come when Angela sent you the e-mail?" I wondered how a distorted mind calculated risk.

"I told myself again and again. *This is a trap!* I wanted Angela to leave the country." He let out a long sigh. "Perhaps deep down, I wanted to get caught. I don't know anymore."

Suddenly, I felt very tired. Controlling my smoldering anger had drained me. Martin was looking at the wall again. It was as if I were not in the room. I stood up.

"I'm not sure I want to see you again. Your twisted cost-benefit ratios have caused me great harm." I walked toward the door. Martin turned and looked at me. His shoulders drooped forward. The turmoil had surfaced in his eyes.

"Don't lose your heart, Larry. I've seen too much suffering." His voice was soft. "I built a wall around my feelings. No wife, no children. I taught you how to make decisions. Perhaps I taught you too well. You have a good heart. Don't lose your heart, Larry." His voice had dropped to a whisper.

I felt like screaming, *Laura was an orphan; she looked up to you as a father!* What was the use? Laura wasn't going to return. I couldn't hate this man. I couldn't pity him either. I needed time to sort through my emotions.

I was just about to leave the cell when a thought stopped me. I turned and looked directly into his eyes. "Remember a line from the Kipling poem you quoted so often: 'If you can bear to hear the truth you've spoken....' Can you complete the line?"

Armstrong had a puzzled look. "Was it 'twisted by knaves to make a trap for fools'?"

"Exactly! 'If you can bear to hear the truth you've spoken twisted by knaves to make a trap for fools.' You spoke the truth in class and God knows you inspired us—but you twisted your own truth to trap yourself in deceit and murder—you were your own knave and your own fool. Somewhere down the line you lost your way."

Then, I had to twist the final jab. I owed it to Laura. "No frame control!"

Martin slumped on his chair as I walked out of the cell. I thought I was done with Martin, but he was not done with me.

20
A Look in the Mirror

Experience is not what happens to you,
It is what you do with what happens to you.
—Aldous Huxley

I had forced myself to clean my apartment. The ritual of putting everything back in place was a way of saying goodbye to Laura. I arranged the books neatly on the table, as Laura would have liked them. I had not only cleaned the dishes, but also put them away in the top cupboard. Laura had always chided me about leaving my dishes lying around. I had scrubbed the bathroom floor and saved Laura's makeup kit that she had left behind. The lemon scent of Pinesol was still in the air. In spite of a warm sunny day outside, my room felt cold and antiseptic. Ten days had passed since I met Armstrong in his cell. Yesterday I had received a letter from him. Phil and I read the letter together:

Larry and Phil,

Larry may be right—perhaps I did lose frame control. In my zeal to help the poor, I did not care about the lives of my nieces. In my mind, the ends justify the means. I don't know anymore. I struggle with my shadows every day—knowing that I have been a failure. I killed two people and I have nothing to show for it—not the result I wanted. As I sink into a hell of my own making, one thing sustains me—the sparks that I have kindled in my students. Students like you, Larry and Phil. I don't rue your success, although your success has resulted in my failure.

I have been finding out about how you solved the case. You learned your concepts well. You were contrarians—who kept asking disturbing questions. You looked at the murder from different angles and reframed the case as you obtained new evidence.

I couldn't make you think it was suicide, although I did fool the police! You discovered my weakest link—Angela. Inducing her to gravitate to her own risk taste was a masterstroke. You sweetened the carrot and kept increasing the size of the stick until she cracked. You understood the role played by the time anchor and switched quickly to a new mindset. You framed me with the concepts I had taught you. I should not have been such a good teacher. Millions of AIDS patients across the world would have benefited if you two had not played the game so well.

I have no rancor toward either of you. I wake up every day not knowing what my life means anymore. I see a dark tunnel with no clear light at the end. Sometimes, many times, a beast sits in my cell corner and growls at me—a beast that I can't shake off from my consciousness. I see him in my nightmares. I can't look this beast in the eyes.

Martin

"Instead of priming the pump, he could say he was sorry," Phil remarked.

"I think Armstrong is beginning to realize that he made some deplorable choices. It may take some time for him to entirely fathom his own folly. He always talked about an honest self-audit of the decision-making process—now he has to do what he preached. At one point he told me that the best way to tame our inner demon is to help others, yet somehow Armstrong couldn't control his own beast. We made many mistakes too, don't you think?"

"Mistakes? Our biggest mistake was not recognizing our biases, Larry. We couldn't separate our values from the facts. We didn't evaluate Armstrong objectively. Our attention was focused on Paul and Donald. Their personalities seemed more likely to be that of a murderer—or so we thought. Only goes to show that appearances can be deceiving."

"Armstrong may be right about reframing. We did reframe the issue quickly. But we made a huge blunder in the beginning: We drew narrow boundaries. We didn't include Diane's death in the puzzle. We were trying to solve Laura's murder, but we missed the link with the mugging incident in Chicago. If we'd tried to figure out the link between Diane's and Laura's deaths, we could have moved in the right direction, don't you think?"

"There are so many 'what ifs,' Larry. Hindsight is a wonderful thing, isn't it?"

"The amazing thing is that the clues were all there, Phil. We didn't pick them up. Armstrong was distracted during the last days of class. He was cool toward Laura when she went to him with a personal problem. He was angry about the handling of the trust fund—instead of helping the poor in Chicago, he wanted to send the money abroad. He was frustrated at not having enough money for his relief efforts. He had a preoccupation with AIDS cases in Africa. In fact, after Laura died, I went to his office to discuss values and facts. At that time he gave me the biggest clue of all."

"What was it?" Phil asked.

"When I asked him how he handled his personal grief about Laura's death, he told me something that I've recently recollected."

"What?"

"Phil, it all came back after I met Armstrong in his cell. When I was talking to him in his office, he said: 'I try to focus on reducing the suffering of others who are in need of help. It reduces my own private pain about Laura's death. I find that helping other people gives me a rationale to be alive—*a rationale to do all the other crazy things that I have to do to help them.* What else is there?' Those were his exact words. He was explaining to me the crazy things he had to do, like murdering Laura! At that time, I didn't really focus on what he was saying."

"You're reading too much into that statement about crazy things, Larry. Don't forget the hindsight bias. You are recalling events selectively. I think we failed to get to the root of the issue.

Remember when he talked about his depression in class? He said he tried to find out the source of his grief. It's obvious now that his frustration was still there in spite of his summer relief efforts. We didn't have a good handle on his motives. We were looking at the conventional reasons—greed in the case of Donald. For Paul Gerber, we focused on his anger and envy. Armstrong's motivation was in a class by itself—it didn't include any personal gain. We had no clue about his real mindset. We were his best students and yet we were out of tune."

"You're right about that, Phil. We couldn't connect the different pieces of evidence because we didn't identify the underlying motive that was driving his actions. We failed to unearth the real causal link that governed his behavior. If we had connected the different threads—his deep desire to help AIDS victims, his ongoing frustration at what he couldn't do, his lack of emotional relations with anyone, his arrogance—we could have gotten closer. Cause and effect is hard to detect, that's for sure. Trying to infer what drives a person's behavior is hazardous at best."

The phone rang. It was Shawn Douglas.

"Is Phil with you? There's been a new development tonight. I wanted to talk to both of you."

"What is it?" I asked, as I motioned Phil to come closer.

"Martin Armstrong tried to kill himself in his cell. Apparently, he swallowed almost sixty capsules of the antidepressant, Elavil®. We don't know how he got hold of the drug. Fortunately, one of the guards noticed that he wasn't moving. We rushed him immediately to the Northwestern Medical Center. They pumped his stomach about an hour ago."

Phil and I exchanged glances. We were both thinking the same thing—the beast had swallowed Armstrong.

"What's his prognosis?" Phil asked.

"It's touch and go at the present. Elavil can cause serious cardiac damage. Depends on how much Elavil was absorbed by his stomach lining. There might even be brain damage. He's still in a coma. Donald is with him."

"When will we know for sure?" I asked.

"Probably within two or three days. The important thing is the neurological exam, if and when he wakes up."

Epilogue
The Heart of the Matter

Reason, ruling alone, is a force confining;
And passion, unattended, is a flame that burns its own destruction.
—Khalil Gibran

"What do you think of the story?" I ask Chris. His hand is on his chin. He is rocking back and forth. The pizza we ordered has mysteriously disappeared. It is 2:00 in the morning, but Chris is wide awake.

"That's one cool story, Larry. The way you guys nabbed the professor was sweet! What happened to Martin Armstrong? Did he die from the overdose?"

"I'll tell you in a minute. But first I have two confessions to make."

"What?"

"The story happened almost exactly as I told you. I kept a diary to avoid the hindsight bias. But I did change some of the dialogues to get the best 20 percent from the class discussions. I wanted to capture your attention. My hook is not perfect—some of the conversations appear stilted—but at least I have kept you awake!"

"I'm not surprised—that's why you kept inserting fragments of the decision-making concepts into the murder mystery...."

"What do you want? These fragments of a story I told you are a reflection of my fragmented life. By connecting all the fragments, I try to derive my own personal meaning. Life may be a tapestry of unrelated random events, but we can imbibe it with our own purpose—seek our own reality."

"Okay! Larry. What's the second confession?"

"I have to admit that Phil Myers deserves almost all the credit. If he hadn't been a contrarian, suspicions about Laura's death would have never surfaced."

"You haven't talked about Phil in the last four years. What happened to him?" Chris bounces on his chair.

I pause for a moment. "Phil was killed in a police crossfire two years after the story. He attempted to rescue a child held hostage in a daycare center. The police sharpshooters were targeting the perpetrator, while Phil was trying to convince him to give up the girl. There was a struggle. He was inadvertently shot. I can't help but feel that somehow the lingering guilt of the traffic accident with Mary Ellen had something to do with it."

"I'm sorry, Larry, that must have been hard on you. How did you deal with these losses?"

"We all develop different types of coping mechanisms. One way to recover is to find some solace in poetry. It's amazing, when I recite my favorite lines from an old poem, the phrases become a source of comfort—a way to heal my bruised emotions."

"What poetry are you talking about? I like the lines you quoted to Armstrong—about how he was his own knave and his own fool."

"That was from the poem by Kipling. The part you like goes like this:
    If you can bear to hear the truth you've spoken
    Twisted by knaves to make a trap for fools,
    Or watch the things you gave your life to, broken,
    And stoop and build' em with worn-out tools.
Martin twisted his own words to justify his crime. I have tried to reconstruct my life with old tools."

"You got a lot of mileage out of one poem, didn't you?"

"You have to let the poem soak into your consciousness—otherwise the lines are mere words. Once you fully absorb the poem—the words become a mirror for self-reflection. A way to assess your inner capabilities . . . to search for the limits of your own perfection. Armstrong taught us how to fully appreciate poetry. The hardest part of this whole episode was my disillusionment with him. The lighthouse that guided my thinking was built on sand—it had crumbled before my eyes. Some of the tools were not only worn out—they were broken."

"What did you do?"

"I had to rebuild my sense of moral order. But initially I had to grieve and recover from the emotional turbulence. Sometimes there is no choice—you have to absorb the impact of the losses for a while. Eventually you have to steady yourself and take charge of what you can control. Look at our situation. Mother has come back from her long struggle. You're doing well in school. I have the challenge of running my own company. We're moving on."

"Why did you decide to tell me this long story today, anyway?"

"As you know, Chris, I'm looking forward to a date with Angie tomorrow. I'm venturing out again for the first time since Laura died. I wanted to take one fond look back as I take a new turn on the road ahead."

"Let's move on with the story, too. Now I know why you keep saying we have to thrive on our stupidity. I'm not sure I fully understand, though. How can we thrive on stupidity?"

"We're all stupid, Chris, in one way or another. Remember what Pogo said, 'We have found the enemy and it's us!' We have to come to terms with our propensity to make mistakes. Try to understand our folly and cultivate it. Manage it effectively. Use its insight to walk toward wisdom. If we ignore our mistakes, they get bigger all the time. We cannot truly conquer our frailties without thriving on them!"

"I think I get it, Larry. It has to do with the long inward journey that you were talking about earlier. What happened to the rest of the gang?"

"After his MBA, Raj went back to his native village in India to help. Clara enrolled in law school. Now she works as a legal aid attorney right here in San Francisco, providing law services in poor neighborhoods. Paul Gerber had some ongoing adjustment problems. Last I heard he was working in a psychiatric hospital as a therapist. John Scott is completing a doctorate in finance at Stanford."

"What happened to Angela?"

"Angela moved to Los Angeles. She brought her daughter from Mexico. She's going to school to become a lawyer. The biggest surprise is Stewart. He has his own multi-billion dollar hedge fund. Turns out, he was trading in stocks day and night. Now we know what he was whispering to his laptop all the time. No wonder he used to nod off in class!"

"What about Donald Armstrong?"

"Donald continues his consulting business. Hiring and firing people is still his major preoccupation. He administers the Armstrong Fund, but he's sent a great deal of money overseas to developing countries."

"You have to tell me now what happened to Martin Armstrong. Did he die from the overdose?" Chris looks directly at me.

"Martin recovered from his coma. Remarkably, there wasn't any neurological or cardiac damage, but he was in a deep depression. He was given a thirty-year sentence in a minimum-security facility. He got better to some extent after two years. He wrote a book about helping AIDS victims. Now, he's working on another book."

"Are you still angry at Martin Armstrong?"

"No, Chris. When I talked to him in the cell, I could hardly control my anger. I was reacting to a deep sense of betrayal. The person I admired most had turned out to be a murderer. Actually, I figured out later that most of my anger was due to another reason."

"What was that?"

"When Martin Armstrong talked about his twisted cost-benefit ratio, I didn't have a good answer for him. His logic irritated me, but it frightened me more than I cared to admit."

"Do you have a better answer now?"

"We cannot justify evil means for good ends. Armstrong emphasized the importance of framing—yet his personal frame had a fatal flaw. Means and ends are cut from the same cloth—they're complementary sides of the same indivisible frame. We cannot do well if we begin with a process that harms. If we compromise on the means, we destroy the ends, too. It is a betrayal of the human spirit. This kind of slippery slope can lead us to the gates of hell!"

"Do you keep in touch with Armstrong?" Chris's persistence reminds me of Phil.

"What do you do with a part of you that has wasted? You can't throw it away. I have spent the last four years trying to sort out and preserve all the good things Armstrong taught me at St. Andrews from the bad things he did—the unexpected betrayal of his human spirit. I wrote a letter to him when he was recovering from his depression. He replied several months later. We exchange correspondence now and then, but the old magic is gone."

Chris stands up. His physical strength seems overpowering. His eyes are that of a child: luminous and trusting. Uncertainty and conflict are *beginning to make inroads. "What should I do, Larry? Which school should I go to? What should I do about Linda? Should we get engaged? Tell me quickly. I'm hungry. I have to find something in the fridge. You still haven't told me what you would do in my place."*

"I can't tell you what to do, Chris. I'm very tempted to do so, but no thanks! I've told you this story because I want you to make your own decisions. Try to create a decision making process and a routine that'll work for you. You need to develop an enduring framework for your important decisions. I've made a list of all the concepts we talked about. I'll help you in identifying the pros and cons of going to work or going to school, but the final decision has to be your own. Do you know what Sigmund Freud said about this?"

"What?"

"Freud said, 'In the important decisions of personal life, we should be governed, I think, by the deepest inner needs of our nature.'"

Chris digests the quote for a minute. "What exactly does that mean?"

"Four years ago, someone told me not to lose my heart. I detested what he told me at that time. For some time my heart shriveled up. Then I left Chicago and came to San Francisco. After a while—a long while— I could feel again. Now I know that it was the best advice I ever received. You have to use your mind to make the best possible decision—but you can also use your heart and your intuition. Your mind can make all the complex calculations, but your heart breathes life into these stale numbers. Learn how to rely on your intuition."

"Gee, Larry! You keep saying 'shine a light into your mind.' 'Embark on the exciting road inward.' 'Trust your heart.' How do you actually go about doing that?" Chris has his hands on his hips. He's so close, I can touch him. In another sense—he is already gone.

"That's the question isn't it? All these issues boil down to the same thing. How do you open the window to your own self-awareness? How do you build this inner sanctuary? A safe harbor to reduce stress—to fully utilize your creative wellsprings. We began the story with how instincts determine our spontaneous decisions. Instincts are a reflex action—a part of our biological evolutionary process. We end the story with the power of intuition—a way of trying to go beyond rational thinking. Intuition can provide useful insights if it's harnessed correctly, but often our subjective responses are highly misleading. We have discussed many psychological biases that cloud our intuition."

"You are saying intuition can be misleading yet I should rely on it?"

"Yes—relying on your intuition may be risky, but it is also immensely rewarding. Two strategies can help. First, we have to fully exhaust our rational process of decision making and ensure we aren't succumbing to any psychological biases. Second, we need to condition our mind so that we can utilize intuition more reliably."

"Again that's just talk, Larry. How do you prepare your mind?"

I point toward my brother. *"The **R**esources **W**ithin are all there, Chris, waiting for you to harness them. A three-step procedure can help us to get there. We have talked about two steps already: **T**hriving on stupidity and **R**elying on your heart and intuition. The third stage, **W**alking toward wisdom, is the most challenging. This has to be your own journey. When you encounter yourself in the dark and silent caverns of your own mind, you have to light your own flame, hear your own music. I can only tell you what seems to work for me."*

"All right, tell me what works for you. Maybe I can learn from your experience."

"For me it comes in stages. You have to learn how to talk to yourself!"

"What? I thought only crazy people talk to themselves. I don't get what you're saying."

"Let me explain the progress I've made in the past four years. In order to walk toward wisdom, you have to explore your own mind and somehow link your inner awareness to your outside world. There are different states of awareness. We're all caught up in our lives, in our relationships, in our jobs and ambitions. You have to learn how to listen to the silence within you."

"What do you mean by that?"

"Listening to your silence is one way of getting in touch with yourself—a way to walk inward to find your own wisdom. Laura taught me how to listen to my silence a long time ago. However, at that time, I never really followed up on it. When we settled in San Francisco, I was thankful for my health and professional life. Trying to start my own software company was a challenge that I relished. Yet, something was missing. My internal chemistry was imbalanced."

"So what did you do?"

"I started listening to myself for about thirty minutes a day—trying to find some comfort in the silence of my own mind. That's the first step—to calm your mind and listen to your own silence. It's not easy.

All kinds of thoughts try to shatter my silence. Sometimes, a current business dilemma, many times, a minor thing that went on at work. You have to let these nagging thoughts pass, and keep listening. I found it difficult to listen to my silence because I wasn't comfortable with myself. I didn't like my own company. But you have to keep doing it."

"What's the benefit of doing that?"

"Once you can listen to your inner silence, you're in a place where your intuition is born—where your mind and your heart forge the very fibers of your consciousness. Although we can never know for sure, I like to think that's what Freud had in mind when he talked about our deepest inner needs. When you ask questions within that silent space, your own creative spirit and intuition bring forth remarkable answers. A tremendous resource opens up to you. You've taken the first big step in your journey."

"What's the second step?"

"It took me almost two years to listen to my silence. Eventually, I could reside in a space where the silence was complete, where no thoughts intervened, at least for some moments. In the second stage, as I became comfortable listening to the silence, I felt a connectedness—an affinity with every other life force. It's hard to describe. It isn't just empathy or compassion for everything around you. It's an actual feeling, an expansion of the spirit, something that changes the way you breathe and your perspective on everything. It's a tremendous release—a realization that even when you die, you're still part of the whole."

"Gee, Larry, is there a third stage after that?"

"The third stage brings you back full circle. Once you hear the silence and feel the connectedness, the world will come roaring back. You will gain a new perspective on your life—tackle your dilemmas with greater energy and creativity. You experience everything with more intensity—yet an eerie sense of tranquility prevails. Some people get this kind of feeling when they know they're going to die. They try to savor every breath. They're more intensely aware of their surroundings. You'll hear the silence, but you'll also hear every other voice."

"What do you mean, 'hear every other voice'? I thought you were listening to the silence."

"I know it's confusing. Sometimes, I feel I'm almost at stage three. At other times, I'm still trying to listen to the silence. The progress is not linear. It comes in fits and starts. I'm learning how to deal with it all the

time. In the third stage, the silence and the noise of the world mingle and make a different kind of music. Very rarely, I've seen flashes of it. It happens when I look at a tree and actually see only the tree, when I listen to the wind and sense only the wind. For a brief fleeting instant, the tree, the wind, and I are part of the same life force. I should stop here. Now you'll think that I talk to trees!"

"No, Larry! I promise I won't tell my friends that you talk to trees!" Chris smiles, then grows serious. "But what about Linda. What should I do?"

"Before we move on, Chris, I want to emphasize that you have to make your own journey. What seems to work for me may not work well for you. Some try to find this kind of awareness in religion, others find it in voluntary service. The three stages we've talked about are three connecting frames. For me these are the ultimate frames for trying to live with a complete sense of awareness—a continuous awakening that gives meaning to my professional and personal struggle. These frames help me not only to reconstruct my reality but also to develop a sense of moral order."

"How do these frames create a moral code?"

"If we achieve a high level of awareness about ourselves and our world, it is difficult to think bad thoughts—let alone harm someone. We acquire an acute sensitivity and affinity to other people's needs. The awareness creates a framework for honest, professional, and personal conduct."

"Didn't they teach you business ethics in the MBA program? Doesn't that help?"

"Teaching ethics will not significantly reduce the extent of corrupt business practices. Schools can clarify the laws and stress the consequences of breaking the laws—but they are not effective in mandating good behavior. Innovative courses in ethics try to encourage a capacity to self-reflect on our own actions—to recognize the fact that in many cases, when the line between right and wrong is blurred, we are often creative in developing different types of rationales to justify our lapses. Although we have an infinite capacity to delude ourselves, ultimately, we are still responsible for our own moral compass. If we are truly aware of the trust and obligations that are vested in us, thoughts of defrauding shareholders by creative accounting techniques are less

likely to arise. Achieving full consciousness is the key to many of our problems."

"*You really don't expect everybody to become a monk, do you?*" *Chris asks abruptly.*

"*No, Chris, I don't. Make no mistake about it—I am not a monk either. I mistreated Angela and contributed to Paul Gerber's paranoia. I have transgressed in many other ways. Achieving a high level of awareness is difficult—almost impossible. I am referring to an ideal we can strive toward. I realize I will never achieve a complete state of awareness. But trying to follow the process releases a lot of pressure—it calms and opens my mind in a different way than exercise relaxes the body. Sooner or later, we need to embark on our own inner voyage of discovery. If we don't begin our walk toward wisdom, we forsake a whole new dimension of ourselves.*"

"*Okay, Larry! Let's get back to Linda.*" *Chris is circling, moving closer to the door.*

"*I understand your dilemma about Linda. You have to answer the question at two levels. First, depending upon your goals, ambitions, and need, try to figure out if you're compatible with each other on a long-term basis. Have a heart-felt talk with her. More important, listen to your silence—trust your intuition. If deep down inside, you feel Linda is right for you—go for it!*"

"*Gee, Larry! Thanks for not telling me what to do!*"

I try to look at Chris's eyes to see if he is serious, but he has already vanished.

Appendix 1
Key Concepts/Questions

Congratulations! Now that you have read the book, what are you going to *remember* and *apply* in your daily decision making? Start with three acrostic phrases:

- **The Wise Can Give New Direction Today.**
- **Begin With Simplicity.**
- **The Resources Within.**

These three phrases can make you **WISER**—an acronym for remembering the five important lessons from the Cicor case study.

Questions are provided to discuss the key concepts in greater detail. These exercises are more effective if they are performed in a group setting with contribution from 10 to 15 participants.

I. The Wise Can Give New Direction Today: The Seven Mantras

The foundation of the novel consists of seven critical concepts that are introduced and applied in the murder mystery. Professor Armstrong will haunt you in your nightmares if you are unable to mumble these mantras in your sleep. They are represented in the acrostic sentence: **The Wise Can Give New Direction Today.**

1. *The name of the game is the frame.*
   Framing is the initial conceptualization of the issue. It includes defining objectives, building alternatives, gathering basic information, and considering what should be included or left out of the problem. Framing is the most important part of the decision-making process because we may inadvertently draw narrow boundaries. We have to conceptualize the issue from many angles to ensure that we have not overlooked an important aspect and try to seek imaginative solutions.

   Be a contrarian—actively look for disconfirming evidence, think outside your conventional boundaries, and challenge your presumptions. (Discussed: pp. 10-14; Applied: pp. 23-28.)

Questions:

   A. Identify three strategies that facilitate your thinking outside a conventional frame.

   B. At your current job, identify three disconfirming questions you would ask your subordinates to find out what they really think about an important issue.

   C. When would you decide to reframe an issue? Identify two specific thresholds that you would consider before you reframe.

2. *Weigh the anchor without rancor.*
   We need to be conscious about our reference points and use them to our advantage. Unfortunately, our thinking process tries to simplify things by latching on to anchors, even when these reference points are arbitrary. We should try to ignore anchors that are not relevant to the issue. But we can also use anchors as an effective negotiation tool. (Discussed: pp. 42-44; Applied: pp. 141-146)

Questions:

   A. What type of anchors do you normally employ when you try to simplify your thinking?

    B. Are the anchors you normally employ arbitrary? Explain and justify.

    C. How would you effectively employ anchors to improve your negotiations about a salary raise?

3. **_Cause and effect is hard to detect._**
Causation shouldn't be confused with correlation or association. Two factors (poverty and crime) may be correlated with each other because of a confounding factor such as education. Higher poverty may appear to "cause" higher crime because less educated persons are more unemployed and have lower opportunity costs. Once we control for education, the correlation between poverty and crime may be significantly reduced or be negligible. It is possible that causation works in the other direction—higher crime rates may result in more poverty. This is a key issue in framing. (Discussed: pp. 51-56; Applied: pp. 127-128)

Questions:

    A. What is the basic difference between correlation and causation? With a specific example, explain how causation is a subset of correlation. What are the other four reasons that may make the two factors correlated, but one factor may not cause the other?

    B. Conventional wisdom indicates that more motivated workers will perform better. In this causal relationship, identify the five possibilities of what might be happening between motivation and performance.

    C. The novel discusses how controlled medical experiments attempt to establish causality by having an experimental group and a control group. Identify three specific reasons why causality may not be fully established in a typical FDA trial.

4. **_Gravitate to your own risk taste._**
Depending upon our subjective preferences and personal circumstances, we are comfortable with a certain amount

of risk taking. If external factors compel us to change our risk from this comfort level, we tend to "compensate" by moving toward our normal risk threshold. It is important to be conscious about the amount of risk we are actually taking and the consequences of the additional risk. (Discussed: pp. 60-62; Applied: pp. 128-129)

Questions:

A. Do you normally gravitate to your own comfort level of risk? Give three examples.

B. Do you undertake more risk consciously with full regard to possible consequences? Identify two circumstances when you have taken more risk subconsciously.

C. How do you normally assess the likelihood of an outcome? Do you actually get some sense of the base odds?

D. What type of subjective biases normally seduce you when thinking about likely outcomes?

5. *Negotiate and trust or go bust.*
Decisions that are inter-dependent lead us to Game Theory. The Prisoner's Dilemma is a one-play game that focuses on self-interest and the importance of trust and cooperation. The dilemma is set up in such a way that if two players look out for their own self-interest, they both end up losing. There are two ways out of the dilemma: Cooperating and trusting each other, or having a binding, enforceable contract. Without these conditions, under the constraints provided by the Prisoner's Dilemma, mutual and individual interest is threatened if we base our decision only on self-interest. The insight is that under some conditions, it is difficult to balance self-interest and common interest. (Discussed: pp. 121-125; Applied: pp. 141-145)

Questions:

  A. Explain two examples of a prisoner's dilemma that are not discussed in the book.

  B. How can the worst outcome be avoided in each case you have discussed?

  C. How would you go about creating a sustainable agreement? What kind of monitoring and sanctions would you consider to be appropriate?

6. **_Deliberate, Investigate, and Evaluate._**
    Arriving at a decision involves discussion, investigation, and evaluation within a framework. A simple framework applies the Balance Sheet method. The more general procedure is WARS (Weighing Attributes and Ranking Scores). WARS can be used for any type of decision making. Scenario Strategies can be used for decisions that are difficult to quantify and involve greater uncertainty. The framework can be modified to suit your needs. Additional complexity in the process should be introduced only if it improves the quality of decision making. Deliberation, investigation, and evaluation should go hand in hand. Evaluate the process you follow periodically by an honest self-audit. (Applied: pp. 67-75, 131-138; 161-163)

Questions:

  A. Consider a specific problem you are confronting today. What is the timeframe for seeking a solution? Who else is involved in the decision making?

  B. For the problem discussed in (A), how long would you allocate for each of the following steps? Justify each allocation.

    - Investigation (gathering data)
    - Deliberation (discussion with colleagues)
    - Evaluation (making actual decisions)

C. How would you ensure that there is a significant over-
lap between the three steps of investigation, deliberation, and evaluation?

D. How frequently would you update your process and
attempt to fine tune it? Explain what kind of decision
audit is appropriate for you.

7. *Track and listen to your feedback.*
We have an opportunity to learn from our decisions. Decision making and obtaining feedback should be part of an
ongoing process. Particularly, for decisions that are
repeated, we need to create a relevant feedback process.
We should be cognizant of overlooked feedback. For
instance, information about projects that we reject, compared to the ones we accept, may be overlooked. Subtle
treatment effects can also impair the accuracy of feedback.
We should obtain feedback while making a decision and
after the decision is made to assess its consequences. Feedback is the key to learning and calibrating better choices in
the future. (Discussed: pp. 105-108; Applied: pp. 151-158,
177-180)

Questions:

A. Do you aggressively seek feedback about your decisions?
Explain how you are proactive rather than reactive.

B. Consider a specific situation in which you get periodic
feedback. Identify some missing feedback. How will
you try to capture missing feedback in this situation?

C. Do treatment effects contaminate your feedback? Provide specific examples.

II. Decision-Making Procedures: Begin With Simplicity

There are many ways to make a decision. Generally, as the
decisions get more important, the procedures will be more

time consuming and comprehensive. We can customize a process to meet our specific needs.

Begin **W**ith **S**implicity. Use the simple **B**alance Sheet method before you attempt more complex procedures such as **W**ARS and **S**cenario Strategies.

1. *Balance Sheet Method*
   This process is more appropriate for deciding between two choices. It entails three steps outlined below. (Discussed: pp. 67-75)

Steps:
Consider an actual situation you are facing between two specific choices. It could be evaluating two locations for your office, weighing two potential investment projects, etc. Work out the following three steps for the problem:

1. Develop the pros and cons of two choices.

2. Weigh the pros and cons by establishing weights.

3. Add the weights on each of the two choices to assess which decision is more persuasive.

2. *Weighing Attributes and Ranking Scores (WARS)*
   Weighing Attributes and Ranking Scores is for evaluating complex choices. This process involves five steps outlined below. (Discussed: pp. 131-138)

Steps:
Consider a problem that has several dimensions. For example: three potential marketing programs or two new product designs, out of which you have to launch one. These are your alternatives or choices. Identify attributes or the pros and cons of each alternative. Work out the following five steps in this comprehensive process:

1. List the alternatives in each column.

2. For each row, decide the weights for each of the attributes according to their importance.

3. Evaluate the score of each attribute for the given alternative.

4. Multiply the weights with the score in each case.

5. Sum the values for each alternative to assess which alternative is preferable.

3. *Scenario Strategies*
    The process of developing strategic scenarios provides a flexible way of dealing with uncertainty, particularly when it is difficult to formalize and quantify the likelihood of outcomes with formal probability estimates. Scenario strategies involve five steps outlined below. (Discussed: pp. 146-149; Applied pp. 163-167)

Steps:
If you are launching a new product, considering an investment project, or evaluating any other specific goal over a span of several years, perform the following five steps:

1. Determine precise objectives, major players, and appropriate timeframe.

2. Identify key uncertainties, driving forces, and trigger events.

3. Generate divergent scenarios based on key uncertainties and driving forces.

4. Focus on the conditions that you can change and identify the interventions.

5. Generate successful robust scenarios based on your interventions.

Each step may take several hours of group discussion. As you begin the steps, the need to collect more information and data may become self-evident. If necessary, repeat each step with more information and input. Monitor the scenario by repeating the exercise with the latest knowledge.

Note: Each of the three decision-making procedures outlined above can be repeated as an exercise when you choose a different context or a fresh problem. Rather than dealing with a hypothetical situation, pick a problem that you are actually grappling with and encourage participation from your colleagues. It will be more rewarding to have a spirited discussion, with diverse points of view, on a topic that matters to you.

III. The Resources Within

Decision making is a hot cognitive process. Your capacity to perceive mistakes, your emotional perspective, and your internal resources all come into play in decision making. Cultivate <u>T</u>he <u>R</u>esources <u>W</u>ithin

1. *Thriving on stupidity*
   Making mistakes is not inherently bad; errors are a natural part of being human. Mistakes provide an exciting opportunity to learn. We need to cultivate an attitude that relishes finding mistakes and learning from them. In order to thrive on stupidity, we have to acknowledge our fallibility and constantly develop insights from our mistakes. (Discussed: pp. 10-14, 183-184)

Questions:

   A. With the gift of retroactive hindsight, identify three major mistakes you have made in the past five years. (Note: If you can't find three mistakes you are not being candid with yourself!)

   B. Within the context of these mistakes, how would you have done things differently if you had to make a choice again?

   C. Have you truly learned from these mistakes? How can you ensure that the same mistakes will not be repeated?

2. *Relying on your heart and your intuition*
   We use our mind (rational analysis of facts) to make informed choices by following a systematic procedure for

decision making. We can customize this procedure based on our own frailties and strengths. But besides exhausting the rational decision-making process, we can gain fresh insights by using our heart (subjective intuition). To do this effectively, we have to be in touch with our inner resources. (Discussed: pp. 185-186)

Questions:

    A. Intuition is to be employed only after exhausting the rational decision-making process. Reflect on two major decisions you made this year. How much intuition was involved in each case? Did you exhaust the rational decision-making process before you used your intuition?

    B. How would you ensure that your intuition is not contaminated by subjective biases discussed in this book?

3. *Walking toward wisdom*
How do we use our inner resources to improve decision making? How do we correctly and effectively harness the latent powers of our own intuition? There is no easy answer to these questions. I have explained one subjective process based on eastern philosophies. Many philosophical and spiritual paths try to do the same thing in different ways. Whatever method is chosen, we need to find a way to be in touch with our inner resources and link them to the outside world. The more we are able to integrate the wellsprings of our inner intuition with our knowledge-based external environment and harmonize the two, the closer we are to a state of full awareness. (Discussed: pp. 186-189)

Questions:

    A. What is the best mechanism to harness your intuition that tends to work for you?

    B. How do you try to keep a sense of perspective and balance in your daily life?

C. How do you improve the quality of your own self-reflection over time?

These are tough questions and only you can respond to them candidly. Your answers to these questions will change as you progress toward wisdom. There is only one constant: If you think you have arrived at the gates of wisdom, you probably still have many more miles to go before you sleep. Part of the wisdom lies in the ability to mount a continuous, life-long search with a realistic dose of humility and an ever-changing perspective.

IV. Lessons from the Cicor Case

Premier Advanced Cardio Enterprises (PACE) and Cicor are imaginary names developed solely for this case study. Any resemblance to an existing company or product is coincidental. *The lessons drawn from this case study are only for pedagogical purposes and should not be construed as a criticism of any existing company or product.* The five key lessons from the Cicor case study can be summarized by the acronym **WISER.**

Lessons: Consider an important decision you have to make at your work or in your personal life. Evaluate how the five lessons of the Cicor case study apply to your particular problem. How can you improve the possible solutions to your problem by these lessons?

1. <u>*Widen the frame*</u>: PACE has to conceptualize the issue in a broad context taking into account the vulnerabilities of the patients, the signaling problem with the doctors, and the approval process by the FDA. If PACE views the problem in a narrow frame, focusing on only its own responsibility, it might inevitably be blamed if patients die because of a break down in the system due to other factors, for instance, doctors ignoring too many warnings or patients not following doctors' advice.

Lesson 1: It is often useful to conceptualize a wider frame for a decision.

2. **In-time information**: The need to develop a mechanism for timely feedback by a centralized database that collects information from patients, doctors, and pharmacists is critical for identifying and addressing problems as soon as they arise.

Lesson 2: It is difficult to make smart decisions without in-time information.

3. **Sample bias**: The FDA trials for Cicor relied on patients who were healthier compared to the patients at large who were sicker and took other medicines. Consequently, the sample PACE had in the FDA trials may have been biased and misleading.

Lesson 3: For any kind of pre-testing, pilot study, or feedback loop, it is critical to have a representative sample.

4. **Evaluating short-term objectives and long-term consequences**: A corporation always faces a trade-off between its short-term and long-term objectives. If PACE pushes aggressively for market share in the short term, without understanding fully the consequences of stronger doses, it may compromise its long-term reputation and viability.

Lesson 4: It is important to weigh all the costs/benefits over an extended time period; the lure of short-term profits or other advantages should not compromise our long-term prospects.

5. **Robust Scenario Strategies**: To develop a viable long-term strategy, PACE can identify the key driving forces and focus on the critical uncertainties to build an overall successful strategy.

Lesson 5: We have to discern what factors we can control and influence to develop robust scenario strategies for successful outcomes.

Appendix 2
Checklist

Decision-Making Checklist

Important Notes:

- Respond to these questions candidly.
- Try to be upfront about your limitations and lack of information.
- Write notes about filling information-gaps and re-working the checklist.
- Ensure that sufficient time is spent on re-framing and learning from feedback.

	YES	NO	N/A

The name of the game is the frame.

	YES	NO	N/A
1. Are your objectives or goals for the decision clearly defined?	☐	☐	☐
2. Have you considered a wide set of alternatives?	☐	☐	☐
3. Are there any other factors that need to be part of the broad frame?	☐	☐	☐

Weigh the anchor without rancor.

4. Are you employing mental thresholds (anchors) to simplify?	☐	☐	☐
5. Are these anchors arbitrary or based on solid foundations?	☐	☐	☐

Cause and effect is hard to detect.

6. Are you assuming a cause and effect ☐ ☐ ☐
    when there is merely an association?
7. If there is a genuine cause and effect, ☐ ☐ ☐
    can you isolate the *net* effect?

Gravitate to your own risk taste.

8. Is the amount of risk you are taking ☐ ☐ ☐
    acceptable in the worst-case scenario?
9. Are you evaluating probabilities based ☐ ☐ ☐
    on objective and reliable data?

Negotiate and trust or go bust.

10. Can cooperation with someone ☐ ☐ ☐
    enhance your chances of success?
11. Will building more trust with someone ☐ ☐ ☐
    avoid a bad outcome for both?

Deliberate, investigate, and evaluate.

12. Are you initially using a simple model ☐ ☐ ☐
    to clarify your thinking?
13. Is your ultimate model complex enough ☐ ☐ ☐
    to incorporate all relevant issues?

Track and listen to your feedback.

14. Have you devised a procedure for ☐ ☐ ☐
    obtaining timely feedback?
15. Have you ensured appropriate ☐ ☐ ☐
    learning from this feedback?

Appendix 3
Glossary

availability bias: We tend to regard an event as more likely if we can readily recall similar events in our "available" memory.

cognitive dissonance: The stress caused in our mind because our cognitive map perceives an inconsistency or is in apparent conflict with the actual situation around us.

confirmation bias: Placing too much emphasis on information or evidence that confirms our prior beliefs.

consensus building: More common ground can be achieved by trying to separate our values from facts. Values are subjective. Experts can shed light on the facts. Disentangling values from facts can lead to consensus building.

defensive avoidance: The tendency to avoid making decisions by denial, procrastination, and shifting of responsibility.

evaluating short-term and long-term trade-offs: Most decisions involve a temporal trade-off between the short-term and the long-term objectives and outcomes. Our decision making should not be myopic: focusing only on short-term gain while compromising long-term results.

frame control: The notion that when exploring different options and trying to think outside conventional bounds, we should not get side tracked and ensure that we achieve our ultimate goal.

gambler's fallacy: The misplaced notion that a random event has memory so that it will correct itself. Example: if a coin tossed repeatedly ends up heads for the first three tosses, the belief arises that tails is more likely in the next toss.

groupthink: An insidious process that may contaminate decision making within groups. It involves cultivating a false sense of invulnerability, stereotyping, and an unrealistic assessment of your opponents.

halo effect: The tendency to view things in clusters and attribute the same properties (or halo) to all the things in the group. Example: a person driving an expensive car is also perceived to be well dressed.

hindsight bias: Our inability to recall past events accurately due to selective editing and self-serving reconstruction.

hypervigilance: An extreme state of emotional arousal caused by stress. Typically we overcompensate or are so petrified that we process information poorly.

ignoring base rates: We tend to rely on our immediate perceptions and ignore objective probability data or base rates.

in-time information: The notion that timely and relevant information is critical for decision making.

M&M (Man and Machine) procedure: It may be useful to combine the input from objective data analysis (Machine) with subjective judgment and intuition (Man). The data analysis can systematically and objectively use all relevant information. Armed with his/her intuition and professional judgment, the decision maker can assess and calibrate the results of the objective model. The M&M method combines the best of both the objective and subjective worlds to provide an integrated decision process.

muddling through: Trying to solve or manage a problem by taking small incremental steps. Most policy decisions involve muddling through. A marginal change is usually made from the status quo after a lot of deliberation.

multiple scenario generation: If we assume an event has happened, we can generate many different scenarios. Once you take the event as a given, many more possibilities are conjured up compared to imagining different scenarios that lead up to an event.

Occam's razor: Also called the *principle of parsimony* named after the medieval philosopher, William of Occam, implies that we should not make more assumptions than the minimum needed. The simplest model is preferred to a more complex one if both the models have the same explanatory power.

overlooked feedback: To have an incomplete picture about feedback, particularly about a relevant group that may not be visible. Example: Monitoring the students you admit to a college, but not collecting the feedback from the students you decide not to admit.

opportunity costs: The costs or benefits forgone for the next best alternative. For decision making, the direct and indirect costs of not following an appropriate decision procedure.

placebo effect: A patient might think he's feeling better when he's taking a dummy pill. This positive thinking may actually reduce symptoms.

post-decision regret: The misgivings we experience if the decision does not have the right outcomes. We either bolster our decision or try to justify it, or we try to follow a new line of action.

random streaks: Systematic patterns can emerge in random events. We tend to pay more attention to these patterns because we have an inherent desire to make sense/order out of any event.

robust scenarios: Constructing successful scenarios that are robust implies taking into account the key uncertainties and main driving forces. Scenarios are robust only if the desired outcomes are relatively insensitive to changes in the underlying conditions.

regression to the mean: The fact that unexpectedly high or low numbers from the mean are an exception and are usually followed by numbers that are closer to the mean. Over the long haul, we tend to get relatively more numbers that are near the mean compared to numbers that are far from the mean.

satisficing: Coined by Herbert Simon, it means that we reduce our cognitive overload by settling for minimally acceptable thresholds or solutions.

sample bias: Any kind of pre-testing will be flawed if there is a sample bias: if the sample does not accurately represent the population at large because of some subtle differences that may bias the results.

sensitivity analysis: The process of checking the robustness of our decision. Assess the sensitivity of the final decision to critical weights and values.

signaling: Many complex choices often involve decoding information signals from a variety of sources. For instance, fluctuations in prices are signals about relative shortages or surpluses. PACE's warnings about the side effects of Cicor need to be communicated as a consistent set of simple and clear signals. Too many shrill signals may be discounted.

split gains and combine losses: Incremental gains and losses have a different effect on our satisfaction. For increasing overall satisfaction or utility, gains should be split up in small portions to avoid diminishing utility. On the other hand, losses should be combined to reduce the overall pain or disutility.

sunk costs: Expenditures in effort, time, or money that are already spent. A decision should ignore sunk costs and focus on new expenditures.

treatment effects: Changes in behavior and performance by a group of people who have been "treated" or dealt with in a different way. It becomes difficult to assess their performance accurately because the group has responded to the treatment.

wide frame: One of the main problems we have in making decisions is that we tend to adopt a narrow frame: draw premature boundaries around an issue before considering a wider set of alternatives and possibilities.

Appendix 4
References/A Conceptual Overview

The literature on decision making is rich and diverse. It spans psychology, economics, and management sciences. All the ideas explained in the key concepts/glossary have been researched in one form or another.

I specify some representative references for further reading and to provide some sense of the extensive scientific work that has led to the development of these concepts.

Books for Further Reading

If you want to read more about decision-making issues, I would highly recommend:

J. Edward Russo and Paul J. H. Shoemaker with Margo Hittleman, *Winning Decisions, Getting it Right the First Time* (Currency-Doubleday, 2002). Henceforth referred as *Winning Decisions*.

J. Edward Russo and Paul J. H. Shoemaker, *Decision Traps, The Ten Barriers to Brilliant Decision-Making and How to Overcome Them* (New York: Simon and Schuster, 1990). Henceforth referred as *Decision Traps*

Decision Traps and *Winning Decisions* skillfully blend economic and psychological issues in decision making. Particularly, framing and feedback issues are discussed exhaustively in these two books and my discussions on these topics draw from them.

Issues in decision-making can be viewed from a variety of perspectives. I provide a representative sample:

Ralph Keeney and Howard Raiffa, *Smart Choices: A Practical Guide to Making Better Decisions* (Broadway, March 2002).

Paul Goodwin and George Wright, *Decision Analysis for Management Decisions*, 2nd ed. (New York: John Wiley, 1998). Henceforth referred as *Decision Analysis*.

Irving Janis and Leon Mann, *Decision-Making: A Psychological Analysis of Conflict, Choice and Commitment* (New York: The Free Press, 1979). Henceforth referred as *Conflict, Choice and Commitment*

John D. Mullen and Byron M. Roth, *Decision-Making: Its Logic and Practice* (Savage, MD: Rowman & Littlefield Publishers, 2002). Henceforth referred as *Logic and Practice*.

Roger Frantz, *Two Minds: Intuition and Analysis in the History of Economic Thought* (Springer, 2005).

Avinash Dixit and Susan Skeath, *Games of Strategy*, 2nd ed. (New York: W.W. Norton, 2004).

Cognitive and Behavioral Approaches
I have taken the view of cognitive psychologists for analyzing the decision-making process and suggesting remedies for inbuilt biases (I draw particularly from *Conflict, Choice and Commitment*). Some psychologists who believe in a different approach may not fully agree with the viewpoints of cognitive psychology.

Since decision making is a hot cognitive process, the emotional aspects are difficult to ignore. There are three issues concerning human nature that are relevant when we make decisions: learning from your mistakes, using your intuition, and tapping your internal resources. These issues are subjective, not traditionally analyzed by academics and professionals, but they are nevertheless critical for improving our ability to make good decisions. I have not done full justice to these issues. However, opening the door slightly and discussing them in the context of how we can improve our decision making is an important step in personal awareness and growth.

The behavioral approach to economics and finance has been gaining momentum. The behavioral viewpoint employs insights from psychology to relax the rationality assumption that is common in economic analysis. *Society for Advancement of Behavioral Economics* (SABE) promotes this approach. Books that have been published recently on this approach include:

Alan Lewis, Paul Webley, and Adrian Furnham, *The New Economic Mind: The Social Psychology of Economic Behaviour* (New York and London: Prentice Hall, 1995).

Gerrit Antonides, *Psychology in Economics and Business* (Dordrecht: Kluwer, 1991).

J. L. Baxter, *Behavioral Foundations of Economics* (Macmillan Press/ St. Martin's Press, 1993).

Peter E. Earl, *Behavioural Economics* (United Kingdom: Edward Elgar Publishing, 1998).

Bruno S. Frey, *Economics as a Science of Human Behavior: Towards a New Social Science Paradigm* (Boston, Dordrecht, and London: Kluwer, 1992).

Shlomo Maital and Sharon Maital, eds., *Economics and Psychology* (United Kingdom: Edward Elgar Publishing, 1993).

Hugh Schwartz, *Rationality Gone Awry? Decision Making Inconsistent with Economic and Financial Theory* (Praeger, 2000).

Richard Thaler, *The Winner's Curse: Paradoxes and Anomalies of Economic Life* (New York: The Free Press, 1992).

Quotations

Thought-provoking quotations at the beginning of each chapter set the stage for subsequent discussions. Two books recommended for a wide range of quotations are:

Jerome Agel and Walter D. Glanze, *Pearls of Wisdom, A Harvest of Quotations from All Ages* (Harper & Row, 1987).

John Cook, *The Book of Positive Quotations*, 1999 edition by Gramercy Books, Original edition: The Rubicon Press, 1993.

The quotations by G. B. Shaw (Chapter 1), John Hay (Chapter 7), Samuel Butler (Chapter 12), Kenneth Burke (Chapter 15), and Khalil Gibran (Epilogue) are from *The Book of Positive Quotations*, pp. 319, 538, 313, 316, and 321 respectively.

The quotations by Will Rogers (Chapter 2), Abraham Maslow (Chapter 3), G. B. Shaw (Chapter 5), Bertrand Russell (Chapter 14), Marcel Proust (Chapter 16), and Aldous Huxley (Chapter 20) are from *Pearls of Wisdom, A Harvest of Quotations from All Ages*, pp. 8, 2, 142, 117, 58, and 61 respectively.

The J. Bronowski quote (Chapter 19) is from the *The Ascent of Man*, 1973. The Francis Bacon quote (Chapter 13) is from *The Advancement of Learning*, 1605. Edward Murrow's quotation (Chapter 9) is from a television broadcast on December 31, 1955. Bertrand Russell's quotation about causality (Chapter 6) is found in his book *The Problems of Philosophy* (Chapter IV, On Induction).

Academic Fiction as a Genre

More and more academic issues are been analyzed in a fictional setting to make the concepts interesting and easier to absorb. Kenneth Elzinga and William Breit, under the pen name, Marshall Jevons, pioneered the genre with books such as *Murder at the Margin* (Princeton University Press, 1993) to highlight economic issues in an interesting way. *The Goal: A Process of Ongoing Improvement* by Eliyahu M. Goldratt and Jeff Cox, North River Press Publishing Corporation, 1992, has been very successful in discussing the theory of constraints in production quality process. Russell Roberts has written an economics primer in the context of a romance between two high school teachers (*The Invisible Heart: An Economic Romance*, MIT Press, 2001).

An interesting book discussing crime and its motive, as well as some decision-making concepts by Dr. Joseph Yassour, *The Zero Illusion* has been published in Hebrew by Zmora-Bitan Publishing

House, Israel (2000). An English translation of the novel is available on the author's home page: http:www.ruppin.ac.il/yassour. Another book by Dr. Yassour, *Decision to Kill* provides fascinating details (based on interviews of prisoners) about their decisions and motivations for different crimes.

Cicor Case Study

The medical facts for the hypothetical case study of *Cicor* by *Premier Advanced Cardio Enterprises* (PACE) were researched from publicly available information on the Internet. Some selected Web sites include:

http://www.fda.gov: **General Web site for Food and Drug Administration**

http://www.ti.ubc.ca/pages/letter24.htm: **For general lipid lowering therapy**

http://www.intelihealth.com: **Harvard Medical School information about statins**

http://my.webmd.com/hw/cholesterol_management/hw115113.asp: **Basic facts**

http://www.mercola.com/article/statins.htm: **About the role of different statins**

http://www.pdr.net/pdrnet/librarian: **About drug interactions and clinical trials**

General information about statins was also obtained from articles in *The New York Times*, *Newsweek*, and *The Wall Street Journal*.

Citations from the Literature

The literature on decision-making issues is extensive and interdisciplinary. Three giants in the field of decision making are Daniel Kahneman, Herbert Simon, and Amos Tversky. Professors Kahneman and Simon are both Nobel Laureates. Professor Tversky's premature death precluded awarding him the Nobel Prize. It's difficult to overestimate the prolific work of these three giants. I provide some representative citations.

Most of Herbert Simon's work can be perused in the following books:

Administrative Behavior: A Study of Decision-Making Process in Administrative Organizations, 4th ed. (New York: The Free Press, 1997).

Models of Bounded Rationality, 3 Vols. (Cambridge, MA: MIT Press, 1981, 1982, 1997).

The Science of the Artificial, 3rd ed. (Cambridge, MA: MIT Press, 1997).

Reason in Human Affairs (Standard University Press, 1983).

Most of the contributions by Daniel Kahneman and Amos Tversky are summarized in two books:

Daniel Kahneman and Amos Tversky, *Choices, Values, and Frames* (New York: Cambridge University Press, 2000).

Judgment Under Uncertainty: Heuristics and Biases, Edited by Daniel Kahneman, Paul Slovic, and Amos Tversky (Cambridge: Cambridge University Press, 1982). (Henceforth referred as *Judgment Under Uncertainty*)

What follows is an account of the key concepts by chapter. I have tried to indicate the references for further reading. An overview of the chapters as they relate to the concepts is provided. Chapters 1 and 2 develop the background for the story.

Chapter 1: Fight or Flight?
The role of instincts in decision making is discussed with the mugging incident. An important distinction is made between information, knowledge, and wisdom. We have more information than we can handle. When we combine information with experience and intuition, we gain awareness and knowledge. However, wisdom comes only if we develop a proper internal and external perspective. The walk toward wisdom is discussed in the Epilogue.

Chapter 2: Thriving on Stupidity

Some general notions about decision making set the stage for specific concepts. All these issues are discussed extensively in the text.

Framing: Kahneman and Tversky define frame as "the decision-maker's conception of the acts, outcomes, and contingencies associated with a particular choice." ("The Framing of Decisions and the Psychology of Choice," *Science* 211 (1981:453). They have shown that the way we structure a problem will change the nature of the responses. In other words, decisions are sensitive to the kind of frame we employ. Appropriate and imaginative framing is the key to good decisions.

Decision Traps (Chapters 2 and 3) and *Winning Decisions* (Chapters 2 and 3) are an excellent source depicting the importance of framing issues. My book draws from their discussions.

Contrarian: The notion of looking for views and information that are different from our own is important. We need to cultivate an attitude that seeks contrary information. We should thrive on actively looking for evidence that contradicts our prior beliefs. Lee Ross and Craig Anderson discuss ways to avoid the confirmation bias in "Shortcomings in the Attribution Process: On the origins and Maintenance of Erroneous Social Assessments" (*Judgment Under Uncertainty*, pp. 149-151).

The notion of asking disconfirming questions is discussed in a corporate setting in *Decision Traps*, pp. 103-105.

A comparison of the approaches used in economics and psychology are discussed in *Rational Choice, The Contrast between Economics and Psychology*, edited by Robin Hogarth and Melvin Reder, 1987, The University of Chicago Press. Herbert Simon's article ("Rationality in Psychology and Economics," pp. 25-41) in this book provides a good summary.

Chapter 3: The Name of the Game is the Frame

Framing is so essential to decision making that I decided to devote an entire chapter on the idea of trying to look at a problem from different angles. I developed the notion of a competition among different frame teams as an interesting way to face the issue in a corporate setting. Note that individuals can discuss their competing frames too.

The notion of Frame Control is discussed in *Decision Traps* (pp. 216-220).

A detailed discussion of framing by Kahneman and Tversky can be found in "The Framing of Decisions and the Psychology of Choice," *Science* 211 (1981): 453-458. The initial literature on framing emphasized that the particular response of decision makers to survey questions is sensitive to the context and wording of specific questions. The framing of questions can change the nature of the results. Mullen and Roth discuss time frames and the social context of framing in *Logic and Practice.*

Looking at issues from the perspective of your own narrow specialization is analyzed in "Selective Perception: A Note on the Departmental Identification of Executives," Dewitt C. Dearborn and Herbert A. Simon, *Sociometry* 21 (1958): 140-144.

Chapter 4: Rewriting the Script
The issue of different frames (and questions) by American and Japanese car manufacturers is discussed in *Decision Traps* (pp. 16-17). Details of automobile production strategies by American and Japanese manufacturers are discussed in the text by James P. Womack, et al., *The Machine that Changed the World: Based on the Massachusetts Institute of Technology 5 Year Study on the Future of the Automobile* (New York: Rawson Associates, 1990).

Chapter 5: Weigh the Anchor without Rancor
In this chapter, we take up the notion that decision making is a hot cognitive process. A good book on this cognitive approach is *Conflict, Choice and Commitment.* My description of patients as reluctant decision makers who try to procrastinate is taken from this book (p. 15).

Hypervigilance: Irving Janis and Leo Mann discuss the positive and negative consequences of this "extreme state of arousal" including the Lord Jim example (*Conflict, Choice and Commitment*, pp. 52-67; 332-335).

Post-decision regret: It's difficult to avoid some form of internal conflict after a decision if the outcomes are not completely to our liking. Janis and Mann have analyzed post-decision conflict or regret extensively in Chapter 12 (*Conflict, Choice and Commitment*, pp. 309-335).

Groupthink: The fascinating concept of groupthink is introduced by Janis and Mann (*Conflict, Choice and Commitment*, 129-133). Other features of groupthink include an effort to rationalize in a collective setting, pressure against those expressing contrary opinions, and different ways of censoring or discounting external views that are contrary to the thinking of the group. Janis and Mann provide many groupthink examples in a policy context.

Anchoring: We may anchor our thoughts to a variety of reference points. The surprising thing is that decision makers continue to use an anchor, even when they are told that the anchor is arbitrary or a random number. This bias was initially discussed by Paul Slovic and Sarah Lichtenstein in "Comparison of Bayesian and Regression Approaches to the Study of Information Processing in Judgment," *Organizational Behavior and Human Performance*, 6 (1971): 641-744. Kahneman and Tversky discuss various examples of anchoring bias in "Judgment Under Uncertainty: Heuristics and Biases," *Science* 185 (1974): 1124-1131.

Chapter 6: Cause and Effect Is Hard to Detect

One of the central premises of scientific work is to try to establish causal relationships. We have a common tendency to confuse correlation with causation. A good method of how we try to rule out some factors that may result in a correlation is in medical studies. In these investigations, controlled, double blind trials are conducted. Note that these studies in spite of their controls do not prove causality.

A good discussion about causality issues is provided in Chapter 5: Reasoning about Causes in *Logic and Practice.*

Placebo effect: The idea of the placebo effect is dominant in the medical literature and is discussed in *Logic and Practice.*

Confirmation bias: We tend to focus on information that validates our prior beliefs or impressions. Peter C. Watson analyzes the bias involving confirming evidence in "On the Failure to

Eliminate Hypotheses in a Conceptual Task," *Quarterly Journal of Experimental Psychology* 12 (1960): 129-140.

Chapter 7: Gravitate to Your Own Risk Taste
Tolerance for risk is a subjective issue depending upon personal preferences, age, and income.

Compensation hypothesis: The fact that we move toward our comfort level of risk when we are forced by policy or some other factor to deviate from this personalized norm is discussed in many different contexts.

G. Blomquist shows that compensating behavior can be utility maximizing if individual and exogenous safety measures are substitutes in "A Utility Maximization Model of Driver Traffic Safety Behavior," *Accident Analysis and Prevention* 18 (5) (1986): 371-375.

Other studies are discussed in H. Singh and M. Thayer, "Driving and Seat Belt Behavior," *Economic Inquiry* XXX(4) (1992): 649-658. John Yun discusses the compensation hypothesis for fuel economy standards, "Offsetting Behavior Effects of the Corporate Average Fuel Economy Standards," *Economic Inquiry* 40 (2) (April 2002): 260-272.

Chapter 8: Murder or Suicide? You Decide
Some major subjective decision-making issues are taken up in this chapter.

Hindsight bias: The clarity with which we normally view past events is an illusion. We tend to filter the information with our biases. For an interesting legal perspective of accurate testimony, see *Eyewitness Testimony: Psychological Perspectives*, edited by Gary Wells and Elizabeth Loftus (Cambridge University Press, 1984). *Decision Traps* (pp. 182-187) has a good discussion about hindsight bias.

Cognitive dissonance: Leon Festinger developed the notion of cognitive dissonance or conflict because of new information and contradictions in *A Theory of Cognitive Dissonance* (Evanston, IL: Row Peterson, 1957). He also points out in a subsequent article that a decision maker that has committed to a particular choice will often try to discount contrary evidence ["Cognitive Consequences of Forced Compliance," *Journal of Abnormal and Social Psychology* (1959): 58, 203-210].

Defensive avoidance: One specific form of defensive avoidance is bolstering: the advantages of the chosen alternative are played up and the disadvantages are minimized. Different ways of defensive avoidance such as denial, procrastination, and shifting responsibility are discussed extensively in *Conflict, Choice and Commitment* (pp. 88-133).

Satisficing: Herbert Simon developed the idea that we look for a solution that is "good enough" or that satisfices (*Administrative Behavior: A Study of Decision-Making Process in an Administrative Organization*, New York: The Free Press, 1976). This concept has been the logical underpinning for other kinds of biases that help us reach the "good enough" threshold.

Decision-making (Balance Sheet method). Benjamin Franklin described his decision process in a letter sent to Joseph Priestly in 1772 (reprinted in *The Benjamin Franklin Sampler* [Fawcett, 1956]). The letter is also quoted in *Decision Traps* (p. 129). The common decision-making process of weighing the pros and cons by a balance sheet is ideal for binary choice, although it can also be extended to three or more options.

Chapter 9: Values and Facts
Consensus building is aided if we try to disentangle the values from the facts. The controversy over abortion by pro-life and pro-choice advocates is developed as an example.

Consensus building: Peter C. Gardiner and Ward Edwards analyze how we can build more agreement if the experts decide the facts and the value decisions are made separately ["Public Values: Multi-attribute utility measurement for social decision-making," *Human Judgment and Decision Processes*, edited by Martin F. Kaplan and Steven Schwartz (Academic Press: 1975)].

Another interesting example of separating values from facts in the context of public safety is provided in Kenneth Hammond and Leonard Adelman, "Science, Values and Human Judgment," *Science* (1976): 389-396.

The framing lessons of Cicor by PACE are summarized in this chapter.

Chapter 10: Shortcuts that Undercut
One of the major achievements of psychological research in decision making has been on the issue of how we process information about uncertain events. Most of these biases are short-cuts to reduce information overload. They are wired into our thinking by evolution. Consequently, we have to fight these biases aggressively; otherwise they can distort our thinking considerably. For good examples about some of these shortcuts in the financial world, see Clint Willis's "The Ten Mistakes to Avoid with Your Money," *Money* magazine (June 1980): 84-94.

A good book on the role of probability and on different policy trade-offs is by H. W. Lewis, *Why Flip a Coin* (New York: John Wiley & Sons, 1997).

Gambler's fallacy: The notion that we try to find patterns in random events is exemplified in the gambler's fallacy, also known as the Monte Carlo fallacy. For a more general discussion of how probability relates to gambling, see Chapter 19 in *Why Flip a Coin*.

Random streaks: We focus on systematic patterns even if they are generated by random phenomenon because we have an inherent desire to seek order.

Availability bias: Events that we can recall or imagine more readily are not necessarily the most likely. Since they are available in our instant memory bank, we tend to regard these events as more likely. Kahneman and Tversky discuss the availability bias in "Availability: A Heuristic for Judging Frequency and Probability," *Cognitive Psychology* 5 (1973): 207-232.

Ignoring base rates: When we rely on our immediate perceptions about stereotypes and ignore the underlying factual probabilities, we succumb to what Kahneman and Tversky dubbed as the "representative" heuristic. "Subjective Probability: A Judgment of Representativeness," *Cognitive Psychology* 3 (1972): 430-454.

Chapter 11: Dissect the Suspects

Rather than trying to project forward, if we assume the final outcome, we can conjure up many possible scenarios. This process of finding more pathways and likely scenarios is important for brainstorming. The halo effect and the regression to the mean are two biases that distort our clarity of thought.

Multiple scenario generation: Deborah Mitchell, Edward Russo, and Nancy Pennington provide a detailed analysis in "Back to the Future: Temporal Perspective in the Explanation of Events," *Journal of Behavioral Decision-making* 2 (1989): 25-39.

Regression to the mean: The fact that values generated (before or after some extreme values) tend to move toward the average shouldn't be surprising. Extreme numbers or outliers are by definition out of the norm, there is a higher probability that other numbers will be closer to the mean.

Halo effect: This bias arises in attribution theory as a special case of the confirmation bias. To view things in clusters and attribute the same properties to all the elements in the cluster are ways of simplifying things (*Logic and Practice*).

Chapter 12: Track the Feedback

The importance of timely and relevant feedback cannot be underestimated, particularly in a dynamic environment when circumstances are evolving. We need to develop instruments that give us accurate feedback. More importantly, we need to learn from pertinent feedback. Chapters 8 and 9 of *Decision Traps* provide a good summary of feedback issues. Overlooked Feedback and treatment effects are discussed in Chapter 9, pp. 189-194. In *Winning Decisions*, feedback issues are discussed in Chapters 8 and 9 (pp. 197-238). My discussion is based partly on these sources.

Overlooked feedback: It's common to have inadequate feedback about a relevant group that may not be visible. We may be ignoring a significant part of the picture. An extensive discussion of overlooked feedback can be found in Hillel Einhorn and Robin Hogarth, "Confidence in the Judgment: Persistence of the Illusion of Validity," *Psychological Review* (1978): 85, 395-416.

Treatment effects: Since we are dealing with individuals in a dynamic environment, treatment effects can be subtle. The treatment effects are analyzed by Hillel Einhorn, "Learning from Experience and Suboptimal Rules in Decision-Making," *Cognitive Processes in Choice and Decision Behavior*, edited by Thomas Wallsten (Lawrence Erlbaum, 1980).

Split gains and combine losses: The basic idea that gains and losses are processed asymmetrically comes from Prospect Theory developed by Kahneman and Tversky, "Prospect Theory: An Analysis of Decisions under Risk," *Econometrica* 47: 263-291. Robert Frank provides applications about splitting losses and combining gains, *Microeconomics and Behavior* (New York: McGraw-Hill, 1998). (Henceforth referred to as *Microeconomics*)

Chapter 13: Verify the Alibi
There is a long tradition in psychology about who can make better decisions: man or a model of a man (an objective model). A representative work is by Herbert Simon and Paul Meehl, *Clinical versus Statistical Prediction* (University of Minnesota Press, 1954). There is a consensus that objective models are better because they factor out random errors made by humans. However, these objective models are typically not able to incorporate intuition and experience adequately.

Decision-making: Man and Machine (M&M): Combining the inputs from the man and the machine seems to work best. For the role of intuition, see Michael Prietula and Herbert Simon, "The Experts in Your Midst," *Harvard Business Review* (1989): 120-124.

The clinical and statistical approach is discussed in Robyn Dawes, David Faust, and Paul Meehl, "Clinical Versus Actuarial Judgment," *Science* 243 (1989): 1668-1673.

Also Einhorn and Hogarth discuss a combined approach with different weights in "Unit Weighting Schemes for Decision-Making," *Organizational Behavior and Human Performance* (1975): 13, 171-192.

Sunk costs: A decision should ignore costs that are already incurred or sunk and focus on new expenditures. Robert Frank provides a good analysis of sunk costs in *Microeconomics*. The psychological perspective is brought out by Hal Arkes and Catherine

Blumer, "The Psychology of Sunk Costs," *Organizational Behavior and Human Decision Process* 35 (1985): 124-140.

The numbers for the hit-and-run incidents in Chicago are guess estimates.

Muddling through: The notion of muddling through is one strategy for satisficing—getting a "good enough" outcome by plodding through a situation. In most cases, one muddles through because of inertia or a constraint, such as a complicated budget process that doesn't allow comprehensive overhaul. However, in times of uncertainty, when new information may be coming in, muddling through may be a desirable strategy. For details, see Janis and Mann (*Conflict, Choice and Commitment*, pp. 33-36).

Chapter 14: Negotiate and Trust or Go Bust

When decision making is interdependent, the strategy one adopts often depends upon what the other side might do. This is the fertile ground for the analysis of different kinds of strategy games. Avinash Dixit and Barry Nalebuff provide a good overview of game theory, including the Prisoner's Dilemma in *Thinking Strategically* (New York: W.W. Norton, 1993).

Prisoner's Dilemma: This is the most common example of a game theoretic analysis. H. W. Lewis provides some good examples in Chapter 7 [*Why Flip a Coin,* (New York: John Wiley & Sons, 1997).]

This chapter provides applications of base rates, causality, and the compensation hypothesis. We shouldn't assess the likelihood of different events based on newspaper or television reports that may focus on sensational events. It's important to look at the underlying incidence rates of an event from the appropriate population. Causality is difficult to prove, particularly in a market environment where there are many players. The compensation hypothesis implies that a person or organization will try to move back to their old comfort level of risk when things have changed because of an external constraint or regulation.

Chapter 15: WARS that Resolve

The WARS method for decision making is simple and versatile. I coin this acronym to represent a generic procedure for making decisions with multiple attributes or factors. If some events are uncertain in the decision frame, the likelihood of these events can be incorporated as an attribute or factor. If the events are, more or less, equally likely, the probabilities can be ignored.

Weighing Attributes and Ranking Scores (WARS): There are many different ways of making complex decisions. I've chosen to discuss a simplified method that can be used for any decision. A more complex version that explicitly includes costs as an efficiency frontier can be found in Chapter 2: Decision-making with Multiple Alternatives (*Decision Analysis*, pp. 15-45).

Alternatively, if we want to eschew comparing options with an efficiency frontier, costs could be included as one of the attributes or factors. A procedure that does not use a cost frontier and incorporates probabilities can be found in Chapter 7 of *Logic and Practice*. Since both sources are textbooks, the procedures are quite intricate.

Chapter 16: Tamper with the Anchor

We normally make a decision based on the information we have collected. It is important to assess the sensitivity of our decision to different values of the key variables since the information may not be accurate or may change over time. If a decision turns out to hinge on some key factors (that are likely to change or have measurement errors), we can try to improve our knowledge of these factors or at least keep an eye on them.

Sensitivity analysis: It's important to check the robustness of a model by changing some key parameters. If the model is sensitive to an important variable, we have to recognize the fact that if this variable changes, our whole decision might change radically. Goodwin and Wright discuss a systematic process of checking for robustness in *Decision Analysis* (pp. 35-37).

Scenario strategies: A detailed method for applying Scenario Strategies is discussed in *Decision Analysis* (Chapter 14, pp. 357-386). The case study of Cicor is analyzed in the context of scenario construction.

Applications of Prisoner's Dilemma and anchoring are included in this chapter.

Chapter 17: Can You Spot Your Blots?
We cannot aspire to be good decision makers unless we are able to face up to our mistakes and biases. The key element is to examine your decision-making process in a constructive and objective setting. If a group is evaluating its decision-making process, it's important to avoid the biases associated with groupthink.

The touchstone for an examination of the process is not consistently good outcomes. Good decisions can result in bad outcomes. It's to examine the extent to which we have used the information available to us in the best possible manner. Robert Hartley provides an excellent comparison of good and bad decisions in *Bulls-eyes and Blunders* (New York: John Wiley, 1987).

The idea that we need to make the best decision by not only following the right method, but also by economizing on time and effort is important. Edward Russo and Barbara Dosher provide a general perspective on this issue in a binary setting, "Strategies for Multi-attribute Binary Choice," *Journal of Experimental Psychology: Learning, Memory and Cognition* 9 (1983): 676-696.

To customize the process for your own needs, we can simplify the method depending upon the circumstances. D. J. Clough refers to the decision about what kind of decision process to adopt as theory of "hyperchoice" [*Decisions in Public and Private sectors* (Englewood Cliffs, NJ: Prentice Hall, 1984)]. A survey of different decision procedures is provided in "Alternative Decision Rules," Appendix B (*Logic and Practice*).

The procedure for decision audits is discussed in *Decision Traps* (pp. 214-223) and in *Winning Decisions* (Appendix A, pp. 267-270).

The lessons for the Cicor case study are summarized under the acronym WISER. A case is made to **B**egin **W**ith **S**implicity and employ Occam's razor.

Chapter 18: The Frame is the Name of the Game
Sensitivity analysis is applied when the decision about each suspect is recalibrated due to a shift in the time of the murder. Since information about the alibis is imprecise, we are dealing

with guess estimates. It's important to realize what we do not know and that key uncertainties may alter the final outcome.

Dealing with ambiguity is a challenging and important topic. For a brief discussion, see Hillel Einhorn and Robin Hogarth, "Decision Making under Ambiguity," (pp. 41-67) in *Rational Choice, The Contrast between Economics and Psychology*, edited by Robin Hogarth and Melvin Reder (The University of Chicago Press, 1987).

Scenario construction is applied when the murderer is framed by the e-mail from Angela.

Chapter 19: What Means to What Ends?
In this chapter, the basic point is that ends cannot and should not justify means. This is of course a very old debate.

Chapter 20: A Look in the Mirror
Phil and Larry recall the clues of the murder mystery. The hindsight bias and the idea of a decision audit are applied. The need to assess our faults candidly is emphasized.

Epilogue: The Heart of the Matter
It's important to use both our mind (rational analysis of facts) and our heart (intuition) in making decisions.

A good book about the dangers and potential advantages of intuition is by David G. Myers, *Intuition: Its Powers and Perils* (Yale University Press, 2002).

Roger Frantz, *Two Minds: Intuition and Analysis in the History of Economic Thought* (Springer, 2005) provides vivid examples of how the analytic mind and the intuitive mind can complement each other in economic analysis.

A three-step procedure for getting in tune with oneself is developed. We can correctly harness the powers of our intuition only if we are in touch with our internal resources. The notion that if we are *fully aware* of ourselves and our world we develop a better moral compass is taken from my favorite teacher Anthony de Mello [*Awareness: The Perils and Opportunities of Reality* (New York: Image Books-Doubleday)].

The story begins with the biological role of instincts and ends with the importance of harnessing the latent powers of our mind—the role of intuition. These two aspects should in no way be regarded as substitutes for rational decision making. Applying logical analysis to improve our decision-making skills is the central paradigm for making smart choices.